A Collection of Management Essays

Joseph WC Lau

Table of Contents

An Overview of the Stakeholder Theory

I believe our philosophy of conscious capitalism will eventually be widely adopted primarily because it is a better way to do business, and it creates more total value in the world for all of its stakeholders.

-John Mackey

The aim of this paper is to have a preliminary review of literature surrounding the notion of 'stakeholder' and stakeholder theory. Upon reviewing a number of key literature, a more thorough understanding of the relationship between organizations and their stakeholders is to be achieved. First, the paper provides an overview of the historic background and development of stakeholder theory. Next, the paper examines the purpose of the theory and how the term 'stakeholder' is defined. Finally, the paper offers a general critique of the theory and suggests areas of future development.

Stakeholder theory is a completing theory of the firm, most well-known for explaining and predicting organizational functions and in regards to stakeholder influences (Rowley, 1997). In his seminal work on stakeholder theory, *Strategic Management: A Stakeholder Approach*, R. Edward Freeman laid the groundwork for the development of the theory. Freeman chose the word 'stakeholder' as opposed to the traditional term 'stockholder' which is more inclined towards an economic point of view of organization. Since the traditional strategic frameworks had been less effective against a more complex business environment, Freeman offered a way to re-define the organization and explain the relationship of the firm to its external environment as well as its behaviour within this environment. Furthermore, Freeman provided a way to conceptualize an organization by graphically modelled the concept of stakeholders as impacting actors on the firm and on whom the firm impacts.

Freeman (1984) stated that prior to his work strategists and scholars hardly consider the significance of stakeholders. Even if they did, the constituents were vaguely defined as 'generic groups' or 'friendly stakeholders'. Major stakeholder groups like competitors or rivals were left out. Further, the literature of that time adopted simplistic if not reductionist approaches for situation analysis; necessary attention for stakeholders' existence were rarely paid. Porter (1980) for example was well-known for splitting the situation up into SWOT analysis. As mentioned by Friedman (2006), an interesting exception was the work from Igor H. Ansoff. Being a key contributor to the strategy literature from the 1960s to the 1970s, Ansoff (1965) defines *objectives* as "decision rules which enable management to guide and measure the firm's performance towards its purpose" and *responsibilities* as "obligations which the firm undertakes to discharge "and not "part of the firm's internal guidance and control mechanism". Anoff (1965) was also a pioneer in stakeholder theory, which the notion of stakeholder theory was originally thought as "decision rules which exclude certain options from the corporations freedom action", such as certain rules or regulations enacted by the government.

In this connection, the focal point behind the Freeman's book was to build a framework that would link the past and respond to the concerns of managers who were being confronted with new uncertainty and challenge. As Freeman (1984) argues:

"Gone are the good old days of worrying only about taking products and services to market, and gone is the usefulness of management theories which concentrate on efficiency and effectiveness within this product-market framework".

As mentioned, the term 'stakeholder', as opposed to the traditional term, is more inclined towards an economic point of view of organization. Since these traditional strategic frameworks were not helping managers anymore to develop new strategic directions and opportunities, Freeman offered a way to redefine the organization and explain the relationship of the firm to its external environment and its behavior within this environment. Freeman therefore provided a way to conceptualize an organization by graphically modeled the concept of stakeholders as impacting actors on the firm and on whom the firm impacts.

Research into stakeholder theory has looked at who stakeholders are, how they impact or are impacted on by the organization. Looking at the definition of stakeholders, Freeman's term is probably the most commonly cited one. In the seminal book mentioned before, Freeman defines a stakeholder as "any group or individual who can affect or is affected by the achievement of the organization's objectives" (p.46). This presents an initial yet very broad understanding of a stakeholder. Therefore, the definition has been contested by some researchers as it allows almost anyone to be considered a stakeholder (Donaldson & Preston, 1995; Mitchell, Agle, & Wood, 1997). Some scholar, for example, calls for a narrowing of Freeman's definition. Clarkson (1994), for instance, argues that stakeholders are risk-bearers and asserts that without the element of risk there is no stake. When combining these definitions, nonetheless, it is reasonable to comprehend stakeholders to include any persons, groups, neighbors, organizations, institutions, societies and even the natural environment who are affected by or influence the activities of the organization. In terms of the purpose of the theory, according to Frooman (1999), the theory enables management to strategically engage in managing stakeholders. Mitchell et al (1997) suggest that stakeholders are group of people who have stakes in an organization and organizations have to decide which of these groups are to be addressed. Friedman and Miles (2006) state that the purpose of the organization is to manage the interests, needs and viewpoints of stakeholders because an organization itself should be thought of as grouping of stakeholders.

Though a variety of stakeholder theory is presented in the literature, a key distinction can be drawn between the theory and the conventional input-output model of firms. While in the conventional model, investor, supplier, and employee inputs are all converted into customer outputs (Donaldson and Preston, 1995), stakeholder theory argues that companies are networks of parties working towards a shared goal and these parties co-operate to create mutually beneficial results. The theory argues that it is salient to identify the stakeholders likely to be affected by or influence the activities of the organization so that consequences of any change in the organization's activities are better anticipated. Besides, stakeholders' 'success criteria' can be identified in order to assure a successful outcome for the organization by building a cooperative relationship with stakeholders.

To further illustrate stakeholder theory, Donaldson and Preston (1995) suggest that there are four central theses related to stakeholder theory:

1. Stakeholder theory is *descriptive*: The theory offers a model of the corporation.
2. Stakeholder theory is *instrumental*: The theory offers a framework to investigate the connections between achievements of various corporate governance goals and the practice of stakeholder management.
3. Stakeholder theory is *normative*: Stakeholders are identified by their interests and all stakeholder interests are considered to be intrinsically valuable. The whole idea a person possesses intrinsic moral rights can be traced back to Immanuel Kant who developed the moral principle of *categorical imperative*.
4. Stakeholder theory is *managerial*: With all the mentioned

aspects in mind, the theory recommends attitudes, structures, and practices to management and requires prompt attention be given to the interests of all legitimate stakeholders.

Stakeholder theory has its strengths and limits. The strength of the theory lies in its nature of being a completing theory of the firm for explaining and predicting organizational function in regards to stakeholder influences (Rowley, 1997). Besides, based on the work of Donaldson and Preston (1995), it is understood that there are four central theses scaffolding the salient functions of the theory. These salient functions are summarised as follows: First, the theory is descriptive as it offers a model of how a firm operates in relation with its constituencies. Second, the theory is instrumental as it offers a tool to evaluate the achievements of various corporate governance goals with the practice of stakeholder management. Third, the theory is normative as it offers an ethical groundwork for how a firm should operate with respect to the welfare of stakeholders being considered to be intrinsically valuable. Forth, the theory is managerial as it recommends practices to management which prompts attention to the interest of all its legitimate stakeholders.

While the theory has its strengths attributed by its conceptual breath and versatility, the limits of the theory arise for exactly the same merit. There are generally two criticisms regarding stakeholder theory. Firstly, as Key (1999) mentions, the current conceptualizations of the theory fail to meet the requirement of scientific theory and modification or enrichment of the theory is necessary. Secondly, the model relationships between a firm and stakeholders as graphically represented by the theory could be oversimplified where more complex dynamics of the relationships are inadequately shown. As illustrated by Fassin (2008), the most obvious 'shortcomings' of theory are that stakeholders can have heterogeneous roles; in addition, stakeholders' inter-dependence and reciprocity may not be as equal and direct as the model suggest. The fact that the theory carries myriad connotations and interpretation makes the theory shy of being specific. The lack of specificity means that advocates of the theory may carry out all the good deeds, but the effects are less likely to be optimal unless these deeds are 'dressed up' with more accurate data and more precise delineation. At the same time, while the theory has a strong ethical connection to business operation, it is highly controversial as to what serves as 'right', 'just', 'fair' or 'moral' along with other prescriptive notions for stakeholders, non-stakeholders, shareholders or an organization. Issues also arise when it comes to who gets the authority to make decisions on various ethical dilemmas and to what extend and degree should a business firm take ethical issues into account when carrying out its business.

Perhaps the most serious problem with the theory roots in the identity of stakeholders. That is, the theory on one hand talks about the fact that a firm contains all these normative or derivative constituency groups, on the other hand, the theory does not have an inclination to address who these groups actually are and the entailed relationships a firm should be having with them. As Fassin (2008) pinpoints, the theory tends to be over-simplified where more complex dynamics of relationships are observed in a firm. Fassin (2008) further argues that the most obvious 'shortcomings' emerge from the identity problem of stakeholders which comprises at least two issues: First, stakeholders can have heterogeneous roles, i.e., the roles of stakeholders could be debatable based on how their identities are defined. Second, stakeholders' inter-dependence and reciprocity may not be as equal and direct as the theory suggest; it is not uncommon to see change of relationship when factors determining such relationship change.

The results of the problem of specificity, particularly identity problem, with stakeholder theory are: First, strategies with the stakeholders are immeasurable as there is too much uncertainty and unpredictability underlying the various domains of the relationships. Besides, when an inconsistency of paradigms exists largely due to the way how different advocates of the theory tend to have different positivist views of the dynamics, it would be contestable in any case once any consensus is made as to, say, what is the best solution or response to the situation. Thirdly, since there is a lack of justificatory framework regarding stakeholder identity and legitimacy, advocates of theory could also take any position they wish in their hands which result in the danger of violating a firm's core business mission and interest due to arbitrary interpretation of, for example, what intrinsic values stakeholders are constitutive of, or how much should a firm 'give in' to stakeholders in meeting their expectations, in some instances giving in for the sake of doing so regardless of what the nature of these expectations are. Finally, the fundamental long term effect of taking the theory with no restrains, particularly, when defining the identity of a firm's core stakeholder hastily and scruple afterwards at nothing lead reasonably to the conclusion that the firm is either being complacent in their business by adopting a general yet simplistic approach for management, or it is simply not willing to take measure closely to the long term effect, tangible or intangible, of such approach.

In conclusion, stakeholder theory offers both moral and practical reasons for management to cater to the needs and sentiments of key stakeholders. Stakeholders are important to a firm inasmuch the underlying rational of stakeholder theory suggests that organizations are obligated to operate with the consent of the community. Nevertheless, in view of the limitations of the theory as discussed in this essay, making reference to the theory with no restrains leads reasonably to the conclusion that the theory is sufficient only when enrichment to the theory is manoeuvred.

References

Ansoff, H. I. (1965). *Corporate Strategy*. New York: McGraw-Hill.

Campbell, C., & Rozsnyai, C. (2002).Quality assurance and the development of Course Programmes. *Papers on Higher Education*. Bucharest, UNESCO, CEPES.

Clarkson, M. E. (1994). A risk based model of stakeholder theory. Proceedings of the Second Toronto Conference on Stakeholder Theory. Toronto: Centre for the Corporate Social Performance and Ethics. University of Toronto.

Donaldson, T., & Preston, L. E. (1995). The stakeholder theory of the corporation: Concepts, evidence, and implications. *Academy of management Review*, *20*(1), 65-91.

Fassin, Y. (2008). Imperfections and shortcomings of the stakeholder model's graphical representation. *Journal of Business Ethics*, *80*(4), 879-888.

Freeman, R. (1984), *Strategic Management: A Stakeholder Approach*, Ballinger, Boston, MA.

Friedman, A.L. and Miles, S. (2006). *Stakeholders: Theory and Practice*, Oxford University Press. .

Frooman, J. (1999). Stakeholder influence strategies. *Academy of Management Review, 24*(2), 191-205.

Key, S. (1999). Toward a new theory of the firm: a critique of stakeholder "theory". *Management Decision*, *37*(4), 317-328.

Mitchell, R. K., Agle, B. R., & Wood, D. J. (1997). Toward a theory of stakeholder identification and salience: Defining the principle of who and what really counts. *Academy of Management Review*, *22*(4), 853-886.

Porter, M. (1980). Competitive *Strategy: Techniques for Analyzing Industries and Competitors.* New York: Free Press.

Rowley, T. J. (1997). Moving beyond dyadic ties: A network theory of stakeholder influences. *Academy of Management Review, 22*(4), 206-221.

Key, S. (1999). Toward a new theory of the firm: a critique of stakeholder "theory". *Management Decision, 37*(4), 317-328.

The Future of Corporate Social Responsibility

All company bosses want a policy on corporate social responsibility. The positive effect is hard to quantify, but the negative consequences of a disaster are enormous.

-Noreena Hertz

The phenomenon of corporate social responsibility (CSR) is often cited in connection with the question of whether there is any "absolute" CSR, or whether, instead, CSR is in some sense merely "a matter of business opinion". Disagreements on how deep CSR should be immerged in a business organization, if at all, remain, and while there might be inconsistencies lurking in this position, it is not unpopular to see an increasing focus on organizations' ethical behaviours and responsibilities (O'Brien, 2001; Waldman, Kenett and Zilberg, 2010). Such organizational shift of focus, advocated by the very term "Corporate Social Responsibility", orientates business organizations to go beyond being profitable and obeying all laws, and commits to avoiding questionable practices and striving for being a "good corporate citizen" (Roberts, Keeble & Brown, 2002;Nelson, 2005; Matten & Crane, 2005). Thus when business organizations are heterogeneous to being the global ambassadors of change and values, how they behave is becoming a matter of increasing interest and importance against the context of global business market and CSR (Hohnen & Potts, 2007). The present paper aims to address the issue of the future direction of CSR and the question of whether and to what extend business organizations should observe CSR practices. The paper will set forth by providing an overview of CSR as an umbrella concept and various definitions the notion is associated with and subcategorized under CSR. This is processed with an analysis of the relationship between CSR and stakeholder theory. What follows is a critique of CSR with an emphasis on the validity, comprehensibility and applicability of the concept. Coming to the conclusion that the notion of CSR is problematic in both entrepreneurial and theoretical dimensions, the paper should attempt to outline the future of CSR being purely an ethical option for business consideration.

The shift of focus of corporations from profits to responsibility is evident today attributed by the dynamics of modern markets. Modern markets not only are highly complex and volatile, but are participated by stakeholders who are much better educated and informed, thus, more selective, sensitive, critical and demanding. The concept of "stakeholder" has attracted a proliferation of definitions; a broad definition probably most widely cited is the one from Freeman (1984): "any group or individual who can affect or is affected by the achievement of the organization's objectives" (p.46).Societal expectations hence arisen which pressure companies to act responsibly with respect to their external as well as internal environments (Du, Bhattacharya & Sen, 2010; Issaksson & Jørgensen, 2010; Waller & Conaway, 2011). In contrast, as argued by CSR advocates, firms that operate with only the profit motive without concern for stakeholders are inclined to show a lack of sustainability (Waldman, Kenett, & Zilberg, 2010)— putting aside for the time being what "sustainability" is supposed to mean. According to Castka, Bamber & Sharp (2004), CSR and CG (corporate governance) are "concepts that allow organizations to operate profitably yet in a socially and environmentally responsible manner to achieve business sustainability and stakeholder satisfaction" (p. vii). While CSR is approached more as a pragmatic question for practitioners (Mackenzie, Garavan & Carbery, 2011), the first and foremost question of CSR remains to be: "what is it"? For it would be arguably unsound and technically difficult to advocate, perform or apply any practices without thoroughly define the premises where these practices are derived from. This is however not an easy question to address inasmuch

13

as it is highly controversial in nature. The controversy of such definition of CSR poises equal difficulty to generality in comprehension and is testimony to Moon's (2002) observation that, similar to prominent concepts like democracy and justice, CSR is in essence contested. Moon (2002) further puts that CSR "is only one of several terms in currency designed to capture the practices and norms of new business-society relations. There are contending names, concepts or appellations for corporate social responsibility"(p.3). These contending names, concepts or appellations may include business ethics, corporate citizenship, sustainability or sustainable development, corporate environmental management, business & society, business & governance, business & globalization, and stakeholder management (Visser,2005). Meanwhile, Sustainability (2004) supplements the meaning of CSR to be "an approach to business that embodies transparency and ethical behaviour, respect for stakeholder groups and a commitment to add economic, social and environmental value" (p.4).

Despite the broad variety of the CSR portrayals as illustrated above, at least one common ground can be observed: CSR clearly has something to do with stakeholders and the management thereof. According to Friedman and Miles (2006), the purpose of a firm is to manage the interests, needs and viewpoints of stakeholders because a firm per se is thought of as grouping of stakeholders. Because CSR and stakeholders are two intertwined concepts, they have been examined and put into a broader assessment of the relationships between business and society (Kakabadse, Rozuel & Lee-Davies, 2005). Considering that a firm cannot undergo CSR without involving its stakeholders, stakeholder management inevitably is to be incorporated as a core paradigm for firms. The mutual reflections of these two intertwined concepts are further elaborated by Donaldson and Preston (1995)'s description of stakeholder theory. According to Donaldson and Preston (1995), there are four dimensions scaffolding the salient features of the theory: First, the theory is descriptive as it offers a model of how a firm operates in relation with its constituencies. Second, the theory is instrumental as it offers a tool to evaluate the achievements of various corporate governance goals with the practice of stakeholder management. Third, the theory is normative as it offers an ethical ground-work for how a firm should operate with respect to the welfare of stakeholders being considered to be intrinsically valuable. Forth, the theory is managerial as it recommends practices to management which prompts attention to the interest of all its legitimate stakeholders.

Matten and Moon (2008) provides another perspective of CSR: "Implicit" and "Explicit" CSR. According to Matten and Moon (2008), "explicit CSR" has the following features: First, it refers to corporate policies that are responsive to societal interests. Second, it may be responsive to stakeholder pressure and may involve partnerships with governmental and non-governmental organizations. Third, it may involve alliances with other corporations when carrying out CSR practices. Fourth, it rests on corporate discretion, rather than reflecting either governmental authority or various institutions. In contrast, "implicit CSR" has the following features: First, it refers to corporations' role within the wider formal and informal institutions for society's interests and concerns. Second, it normally consists of values, norms, and rules defined in collective terms that result in requirements for corporations to address stakeholder issues. Third, while firms would often be directly involved in these requirements, individual corporations would not normally articulate their own versions of such responsibilities. Hence, while Matten and Poon (2008)'s delineation of CSR into being "implicit" and "explicit" help conceptualize the definition and legitimization of CSR in a relatively pragmatic sense, the notion of "stakeholder" is once again engaged which further reinforces the importance of such notion in contemplating CSR in general.

Nevertheless, should stakeholder theory is identified to be the only thread that connects all the portrayals of CSR, then the understanding of CSR is inclined towards the realm of lack of specificity, certainty and endorsement. As a number of studies have pointed out, one major criticism of stakeholder theory is its lack of specificity as to what scope the theory entails and what identities do various stakeholders hold (Kakabadse, Rozuel and & Lee-Davies, 2005). According to Key (1999), the theory falls short of fulfilling the requirements of scientific theory, and modification or enrichment of the theory is necessary. Hence, in case CSR is argued in a way such that corporations are "socially responsible" or should hold accountability to all their legitimate stakeholders, then the whole idea becomes valueless because it is too broad on one hand and means nothing from a managerial point of view on the other (Hummels, 1998; Vinten, 2000). So while opinions continue to diverge as to what exactly CSR stands for and how it should be perceived, Bocholt and Carroll (2012) offer a four-part definition:

> The social responsibility of business encompasses the economic, legal, ethical, and discretionary (philanthropic) expectations that the society has of organizations at a given point in time (p. 34)

Such definition is stemmed from the original definition from Carroll (1983) which is one of the most widely accepted and cited (Crane & Matten, 2004; Harjanne, 2010):

> The conduct of a business so that it is economically profitable, law abiding, ethical and socially supportive. To be socially responsible then means that profitability and obedience to the law are foremost conditions when discussing the firm's ethics and the extent to which it supports the society in which it exists with contributions of money, time and talent (p. 608)

It is not without irony that even as popular as Carroll (1983)'s definition of CSR, by Carroll's (1999) own admission, it is only one of countless definitions which have proliferated in the literature since the 1950s. In fact, back in the 1970s, Friedman (1970) simply suggests that:

> There is one and only one social responsibility of business—to use its resources and engage in activities designed to increase its profits so long as it says within the rules of the game, which is to say, engages in open and free competition without deception or fraud (p. 6)

While it opens to debate whether Friedman's "play-by the-rules" or Carroll's CSR Pyramid may be the best model for CSR (Visser, 2005), before any conclusion or consensus are ever reached, the way how CSR has been defined, as that from Carroll or Sustainability, entails a trend of describing not merely "what CSR is" but "why CSR is necessary". Such trend transcends a managerial concept into a positivist theory of normative actions for corporations, attributing a necessity in turns, giving companies obviously few reasons to refute and retreat back to the common ground of probability and legality. Taken CSR for granted, some advocates of CSR like Smith (2002) asserts that CSR is not a question of *whether* companies should engage, but *how to engage*. Along the same line of rational, we have Elkington (1998)'s concept of "triple bottom-line"—economic, social, and environmental for CSR, not for consideration of whether but for realization of the drivers behind CSR initiatives for modern companies. Among other drivers of CSR, Weyzig (2007) finds that some CSR initiatives are supported by political and economic arguments, but Levy and Kaplan (2007) put more emphasis on the political-strategic aspects of CSR initiatives. Asongu (2007) discovers a link between CSR and innovation and recommends that CSR should be considered as an investment rather than an expense. Participation in the activities of CSR and CSI (Corporate Social Investment), as some CSR advocates would hold, contribute to positive social transformation and benefit participating business organizations themselves (Ndhlovu, 2009).

So it seems CSR is *the* irrefutable answer and irrevocable direction for business corporations, but is it? Looking at the overwhelming arguments for CSR, still, we would have to accept the fact that the construct of CSR lies heavily in a configuration of social-critical theory rather than a scientific one (Scherer & Palazzo,2007; Kuhn& Deetz as quoted in Crane et al, 2008). In this light, while there could be empirical research for enhancing the validity and soundness of various initiatives, the fundamental question remains to be the fact that when interpreting these data, we cannot draw any conclusion farther than an ethical connection to business operation. And drawing such ethical connection is constructive on one hand, yet it is meaningless on the other hand due to its highly controversial nature to the moral knowledge of what serves as 'accountable, 'responsible', 'substantial' or 'moral' along with other prescriptive notions for stakeholders, non-stakeholders, shareholders or an organization. Issues also arise when it comes to who gets the authority to make decisions on various ethical dilemmas and to what extend and degree should a business firm take ethical issues into account when carrying out its business. Zamagni (2012) observes that CSR has no commonly accepted definition and it is at the oxymoronic phase of "privatization" of the definition. Even if there were a "privatized" definition of CSR, it would make sense only if it becomes a common property of a scientific community (Zamagni, 2012). Therefore, the critique for CSR emerges and poises contemplation towards the other side of, once again, the key question "What is it".

In an extensive work conducted by Oosterhout and Heugens (2006), CSR is referred as a "conceptual epiphenomenon" (p. 34). Oosterhout and Heugens (2006) argue that the notion of CSR is largely an insignificant by-product of other conceptual schemes that can "safely be removed from all future theorizing in management and organization...business and society scholars do so without further ado." (p. 34). According to Oosterhout and Heugens (2006), a broad range of activities that were previously recognized under diffuse labels are now conveniently rubricated under the more encompassing header of CSR. Oosterhout and Heugens (2006) further argues that no satisfactory intentional definition of CSR has been found and the concept of CSR is challenged by operationalisation problems. The four operationalisation problems as outlined by Oosterhout and Heugens (2006) suggest in particular that using the prevalent CSP (corporate social performance) as the empirical manifestation of a firm's social responsibility is inclined to be worthless. The four operationalization problems are summarized as follows: first, *negative extensionality* which refers to the problematic screening approach in determining the extension of CSP (corporate social performance). Second, *under inclusiveness* which says the CSP measurement of single-item nature is flawed because of the limited validity and reliability of the test scores it yields. Third, *category lumping* which refers to the problem of many multiple-item CSP measures as simple aggregation techniques may destroy essential information concerning firms' CSP profile and result in non-sensible measures. Finally, *outcome fetishism* which says many output-focused CSP measures are faulty because the fundamental transformation processes behind good or bad CSP outcomes can blind the results. Therefore, Oosterhout & Heugens (2006) conclude that a firm can neither take CSR theory building nor empirical research on CSR very seriously and what seals CSR's fate "is the notion's redundancy in both positive and normative theorizing in business and society." (p. 33)

While Oosterhout & Heugens (2006) emphasize the conceptual-empirical limitations of CSR, Fauset (2006) focuses on the managerial shortcomings of CSR. Fauset (2006) holds that CSR helps "greenwash" the company's image and cover up negative impacts by saturating the media with positive images of the company's CSR credentials. Fauset (2006) further argue that should CSR be treated as a managerial option, it would be problematic because: first, since companies cannot act in any wider interest than making profit for their shareholders, CSR is of limited use in creating social change. Besides, since CSR is considered to be a vehicle for companies to control corporate power and gain access to markets, CSR is a problem not a solution. Third, a critique of corporate power at their heart and a will to dismantle corporate power is the prerequisite for firms to control their destructive impacts; otherwise they reinforce rather than challenge power structures, and undermine popular struggles for autonomy, democracy, human rights and environmental sustainability. Finally, Fauset (2006) asserts that CSR is the wrong strategy and proposes five solutions for rectifying the struggles of firms: First, set regulation to achieve a shift of power. Second, encourage grassroots action and international solidarity to fight against corporate abuse. Third, challenge the expansion of corporate power by the efforts of all stakeholders. Fourth, expose the corporation and dismantle the propaganda people are driven to believe. Fifth, build alternatives and enhance people's autonomy for creating new social order in the shell of the old.

Comparing Oosterhout & Heugens (2006) with Fauset (2006) on the criticism of CSR, there are three differences observed: First, Oosterhout & Heugens (2006) suggest that a firm should forfeit CSR altogether because it is conceptually flawed, while Fauset (2006) suggest that a firm should not blind themselves in believing CSR as the right choice for ethical practice. Second, Oosterhout & Heugens (2006) stress on the lack of empirical support for CSR definition, while Fauset (2006) points out how CSR may result in just the opposite of an ethical intention. Third, Oosterhout & Heugens (2006) imply that CSR should not be taken seriously as it is just a fuzzy, incoherent concept, while Fauset (2006) imply that corporate responsibility or accountability is not unimportant yet the conventional approaches or strategies adopted by companies are not close to being effective and ideal in terms of social responsibility. Concurring with Fauset (2006), Nijhof & Jeurissen (2010) see that CSR has evolved into a marketable asset of companies, but such "commodification" of CSR has at a considerable price from the perspective of the social responsibility of business where opportunism, intact institutional blockades intact and null intrinsic motivation for engaging in CSR result. Nijhof & Jeurissen (2010) however does not hold that CSR is not totally worthless for companies; it just a "glass ceiling" of CSR where inherent limitations are created by companies' business case approach towards CSR. As recommended by Nijhof & Jeurissen(2010), in order to shatter the glass ceiling, business leaders should not to fall back to ethical idealism, yet they should reflect on what ethical guidelines are appropriate in good and bad times and use this commitment as a foundation for developing business models that are also economically sustainable.

Nijhof & Jeurissen(2010) imply that the possibility of a business approach to CSR is sound only if there is a sincere commitment towards assembling ethical guidelines which a company is comfortable with. Otherwise, let alone CSR policies with any business approaches, the construct of CSR is inherently full of dilemmas and challenges which form a glass ceiling. Comparable to Nijhof & Jeurissen(2010), Wagner, Lutz&Weitz (2009) point to the fact that inconsistent CSR information can trigger consumers' perceptions of corporate hypocrisy and thus jeopardize their positive CSR beliefs and attitudes toward the firm. In specific, Wagner et al. (2009) argue that proactive CSR strategies may inherent a risk if they convey a firm's standards of social responsibility, which may be followed by the revelation of actions violating such principles. Reactive CSR strategies are frequently employed by firms to combat the negative consequences of negative CSR behaviours reported, but the more reactive CSR strategies are observed, the more it leads to customers' perceptions of corporate hypocrisy (Wagner et al., 2009). Therefore, even as advocates of CSR would hold, it would be injudicious to simply run CSR without consideration of the inherent challenges, complexity, complications and conflicts.

Considering that it is controversial as to whether or not the "invisibly hand" of CSR really has anything to do with profit or being legitimate as a business approach (Garriga & Melé, 2004; Tsoutsoura, 2004; White, 2006), since the problems of CSR remain to be unresolved, in particular, its validity and comprehensibility, any further effort in postulating the applicability of the notion is a waste of effort. In this regard, CSR has no alternative but to be considered as a non-economic model for firms. The epistemology of CSR, as that of any moral notions, entice as a norm a widespread disagreement among experts which affects knowledge or comprehensibility before any judgment is made (McGrath, 2008; Christensen2009). Elga (2006) in defending a view articulated in the epistemology literature as the "the equal weight view"[1], reasons that if two parties arrive at different answers of the same issue, one party is required to suspend judgment. According to Elga (2006), while on one hand the equal weight view seems to have far-reaching sceptical consequences, on the other hand, it is a strategy to maintain one's objectivity by taking into account the cluster of related issues as a single compound issue, and hastily penalizing the so-called false views about the surrounding issues, hence, the case for scepticism is restored. Putting CSR in perspective, does it not hold true that the future of CSR lies, not in further advancing in a perverse manner, but in taking a step back for cooling down and have a rethinking of the concept. In order to prevent CSR being further promoted hastily as a modern economic approach or ethical idealism for business organizations, it is necessary for business

[1] The equal weight view proposes that one is required to give equal weight to the judgment of a disagreeing epistemic peer as to one's own judgment reasoning about the issue

leaders to consider it objectively only as a moral notion in every sense of the meaning, and make readily available as a business option for consideration, moderation and application.

In conclusion, the concept of CSR contains unresolved difficulties in terms of validly and comprehensibility. There are charming words loaded with enthusiasm and idealism, but in any case, the notion fails to offer fundamental proof to why it is something that a firm cannot live without or a universal law to how companies should abide to. In case companies argue that CSR strategies are to be determined in a fashion of depends-on-situation, then it falls inevitably into managerial arbitrariness which is wide open to interpretation and controversies. In case questionable practices of modern corporations are to be glossed up altogether conveniently by a questionable notion, it raises more ethical problems in fact than it intended to solve. What looks slick in appearance yet rusted inside risk business leaders in revealing their cynical yet hypocritical nature, sooner or later; more dangerous for stakeholders in the society as they put forth their trust and faith in many of these business organizations. Are they indeed "responsible", "accountable" or "just" is not to be determined just by some CSR awards gained or some random acts of the Samaritans. It is mentioned in this paper that wash back of customers is possible when they realize the impact of negative CSR actions of firms. Customers are more educated nowadays and firms have to be vigilant about what they consider to be "CSR-Pro" not a case of doing so for the sake of doing so. Without persuading themselves any higher virtuous meanings of their actions more than sheer business values, inclined quite likely with contrived motives, a business organization is not advocating corporate social responsibility but "irresponsibility". Finally, therefore, a moral evolution in the discovery of true CSR is necessary which would guide business organizations away from mitigating "sins" in the first place.

Reference

Archie B. Carroll and Ann K. Bocholt, *Business and Society - Ethics and Stakeholder Management*, 7th Edition (2012), South-Western Engage

Asongu, J. J. (2007). Innovation as an argument for corporate social responsibility. *Journal of Business and Public Policy, 1*(3), 1-21.

Carroll, A. B. (1983).Corporate social responsibility: Will industry respond to cut-backs in social program funding? *Vital Speeches of the Day,* 49, p. 604-608.

Carroll, A. B. (1999). Corporate social responsibility. *Business and Society,* 38[3], p. 268-295.

Castka, P., Bamber, C., & Sharp, J. M. (2004). *Implementing Effective Corporate Social Responsibility and Corporate Governance.* A Framework. BSI British Standards Institution.

Christensen, D. (2009). Disagreement as evidence: The epistemology of controversy. *Philosophy Compass, 4*(5), 756-767.

Crane, A. & Matten, D. (2004). *Business Ethics.* Oxford: Oxford University Press.

Crane, A., McWilliams, A., Matten, D., Moon, J., & Siegel, D. S. (Eds.). (2008). *The Oxford handbook of corporate social responsibility.* OUP Oxford.

Donaldson, T. & Preston, L. 1995. The stakeholder theory of the modern corporation: Concepts, evidence and implications. *Academy of Management Review* 20, 65-91

Du, S., Bhattacharya, C. B., & Sen, S. (2010). Maximizing business returns to corporate social responsibility (CSR): The role of CSR communication. *International Journal of Management Reviews,* 12(1), 8-19.

Elga, A. (2007). Reflection and disagreement. *Noûs, 41*(3), 478-502.

Elkington, J. (1998). *Cannibals with forks: The triple bottom line of 21st century business.* Gabriola Island, BC: New Society Publishers.

Fauset, C. (2006): *What's wrong with CSR?* Corporate Watch Report.

Friedman, M. (1970). The social responsibility of business is to increase its profits. *New York times magazine,* 13(1970), 32-33.

Friedman, A. L., & Miles, S. (2006). *Stakeholders: Theory and practice.* Oxford University Press

Freeman, R. (1984), *Strategic Management: A Stakeholder Approach,* Ballinger, Boston, MA.

Gjølberg, M. (2009). Measuring the immeasurable?: Constructing an index of CSR practices and CSR performance in 20 countries. *Scandinavian Journal of Management, 25*(1), 10-22.

Garriga, E., & Melé, D. (2004). Corporate social responsibility theories: mapping the territory. *Journal of business ethics,* 53(1-2), 51-71.

Harjanne, P. (2010). Employees as stakeholders in international CSR reporting: a case country comparison.

Hohnen, P., & Potts, J. (2007). Corporate Social Responsibility. *An Implementation Guide for Business. International Institute for Sustainable Development.*

Hummels, H. (1998) 'Organizing ethics: a stakeholder debate', *Journal of Business Ethics,* Vol. 17, Iss. No. 13.

Isaksson, M. and Jørgensen, P.E. (2010). Communicating Corporate Ethos on the Web: The Self-Presentation of PR Agencies. *Journal of Business Communication,* 47(2), 119-140. Doi: 10.1177/0021943610364516

Kakabadse, N. K., Rozuel, C., & Lee-Davies, L. (2005). Corporate social responsibility and stakeholder approach: a conceptual review. *International Journal of Business Governance and Ethics, 1*(4), 277-302.

Key, S. (1999). Toward a new theory of the firm: a critique of stakeholder "theory". *Management Decision, 37*(4), 317-328.

Levy, D., & Kaplan, R. (2008). CSR and theories of global governance: strategic contestation in global issue arenas. *The Oxford Handbook of Corporate Social Responsibility, Oxford: Oxford University Press, forthcoming.*

Mackenzie, C., Garavan, T., & Carbery, R. (2011). Corporate social responsibility: HRD as a mediator of organizational ethical behavior. In *12th international HRD conference, University of Gloucestershire, in Cheltenham, UK.*

Matten, D., & Crane, A. (2005). Corporate citizenship: toward an extended theoretical conceptualization. *Academy of Management review, 30*(1), 166-179.

Matten, D., & Moon, J. (2008). "Implicit" and "explicit" CSR: A conceptual framework for a comparative understanding of corporate social responsibility. *Academy of Management Review, 33*(2), 404-424.

McGrath, S. (2008). Moral disagreement and moral expertise. *Oxford Studies in Metaethics, 3,* 87-108.

Moon, J. (2002). Corporate social responsibility: an overview. *International Directory of Corporate Philanthropy,* 3-14.

Ndhlovu, T. P. (2009). Conceptualizing corporate social responsibility and corporate social investment: The South African context. In *IAABD Conference Paper* (pp. 19-23).

Nelson, J. (2005). *Corporate citizenship in a global context. CSRI Working Paper, 13,* Harvard University.

Nijhof, A. H., & Jeurissen, R. J. (2010). The glass ceiling of corporate social responsibility: Consequences of a business case approach towards CSR. *International Journal of Sociology and Social Policy*, *30*(11/12), 618-631

O'Brien, D. (2001). Integrating corporate social responsibility with competitive strategy. *The Center for Corporate Citizenship at Boston College*, 3-23..

Roberts, S., Keeble, J., & Brown, D. (2002).The business case for corporate citizenship. *Arthur D. Little, Ltd.*, Cambridge, UK, 8.

Scherer, A., & Palazzo, G. (2007). Toward a Political Conception of Corporate Responsibility-Business and Society Seen from a Habermasian Perspective. *Academy of Management Review*, *32*, 1096-1120.

Smith, N. C. (2003). Corporate Social Responsibility: not whether, but how. *Center for Marketing Working Paper*, (03-701).

Sustainability (2004). Gearing Up: From Corporate Responsibility to Good Governance and Scaleable Solutions. London: Sustainability.

Tsoutsoura, M. (2004). Corporate social responsibility and financial performance.

Van Oosterhout, H., & Heugens, P. (2006).Much ado about nothing: a conceptual critique of CSR. *ERIM Research in Management, ERIM Report Series Reference No. ERS-2006-040-ORG. Available at SSRN: http://ssrn.com/abstract=924505*

Vinten, G. (2000) 'The stakeholder manager', Management Decision, Vol. 38, Iss. No. 6, pp.377–383.

Visser, W. (2006). Revisiting Carroll's CSR pyramid. *Corporate Citizenship in Developing Countries*, 29-56.

Wagner, T., Lutz, R. J., & Weitz, B. A. (2009). Corporate hypocrisy: Overcoming the threat of inconsistent corporate social responsibility perceptions. *Journal of Marketing, 73*(6), 77-91.

Waldman, D., Kenett, R. S., & Zilberg, T. (2010). Corporate Social Responsibility: What it really is, Why it's so important, and How it should be managed. *School of Global Management and Leadership, Arizona State University.*

Waller, R.L. and Conaway, R.N (2011). Framing and Counterframing the Issue of Corporate Social Responsibility: The Communication Strategies of Nikebiz.com. *Journal of Business Communication,* 48(1), 83-106. Doi: 10.1177/0021943610389752

Weyzig, F. (2009). Political and economic arguments for corporate social responsibility: Analysis and a proposition regarding the CSR agenda. *Journal of Business Ethics, 86*(4), 417-428.

White, A. L. (2006). Business brief: Intangibles and CSR. *Business for Social Responsibility.*

Zamagni, S. (2012). The ethical anchoring of corporate social responsibility and the critique of CSR. In *Free Markets and the Culture of Common Good* (pp. 191-207). Springer , Netherlands.

Adopting the Right Changing Culture

Slowness to change usually means fear of the new.
— Philip Crosby

In today's business environment where globalisation has a strong impact, change is the only thing being unchanged. For an organisation to best satisfy consumer wants and be profitable, management is expected to be heads up on the pressure and forces raging from all directions and take the necessary measures for change. In terms of how organisations should go about change, there is a divergence of opinion among commentators: some argue that organisations must be willing to undertake rapid change which is by nature 'painful', while others argue that change can be introduced in a relatively 'painless' way. Which of these claims is more relevant to today's business environment?

Rapid change to an organisation is like breaking an ice-cube with a pickaxe, generally referred as 'transformational change'. An organisation has her period of growth and success plateau which may not last forever. When chaos emerges and wake up calls appear, old state and mind-set are in position to shift. The organisation would have to either pass through the 'bottle neck' and re-emerge or simply perish. According to Want (1993), drastic change should involve dramatically reshaping the competitive capabilities of entire industries. Drastic change is also done through visioning and learning in a process which is usually painful. Inasmuch individuals, despite knowing how important change is, are easily irritated and upset by it. Uncertainty is intimidating at the same time when it comes to upsetting the process and practice and affecting the status quo. Therefore, individuals would cling to the past so as to prevent any disturbance to core habits and routines. But it is a do or die situation and time waits for nobody.

On the contrary, painless change is like melting an ice-cube naturally in its own course, generally referred as 'transitional change.' An organisation has the need to dismantle her old state of operation and develop a more effective new state within an agreed upon timetable. Inasmuch the process is not an 'overnight' sabotage of the obsolete system; individuals have the time and psychological preparation adapting to the change. According to Abrahamson (2000), a dynamic stability of the organisation is to be maintained when an organisation adopts change that involves the reconfiguration of existing practices and business models rather than creation of new ones. Resistance from stakeholders, pressures from the environment, stress from implementation could all be dealt with incrementally and reduce impact to the lowest threshold possible. Resistance is also more effectively catered because there is sufficient time for premeditated survey and establishment of preventive measures

Globalisation in today's business environment is highlighted by its complex dynamics and abundant technology. It is also an era where business is conducted with less boundaries, and competition is cultivated by collaborating across time, distance, organization and culture (Marković, 2008). Compared to the past which was more static and predictable, the present is far more fast-paced and unstable. Since more competitors are involved in the business environment and operation is carried out with better efficiency, management of an organisation must have the capability to respond in an unimpeded fashion. A fundamental shift in the organisation's culture and people's behaviour and mind-sets are mandatory so as to implement the necessary change and achieve the new state. It is only with the formation of a new state before an organisation's destination is fully understood and defined, thus assure compatibility, longevity and prosperity. Dunphy and Stace (1993) recognise the traditional organisational model where incremental change combined with a participative management style is inadequate and unrepresentative of how change in many contemporary organisations is actually carried out. In fact, most organisations studied by Dunphy and Stace (1993) show that an organisation development is better represented by transformational change with a directive leadership style. Furthermore, with respect to a system approach of effective change management, the key is to ensure the change of the internal system matches that of the external environment—the scenarios are not unapparent to articulate: When you don't change as rapidly as the environment, you fail. When you can change as fast as the environment, you keep the game going. When you have the foresight to change and make the right decision ahead of the environment, you win. Hence, while responding swiftly to the need of change is one salient feature of good leadership; better when the leader has the competence to stand high and see far. Landrum, Howell, and Paris (2000) describes great leaders as those who always put in charge of any change strategy with the capability of communicating a vision and mobilizing the energy necessary for a turnaround

Should a company fail to respond to the need of rapid change, or be unable to reconcile the internal system to the external environment, tragedy results. This could be illustrated by the classic case of Wang Laboratories. Wang Laboratories was founded in 1951 by Dr. An Wang and Dr. G. Y. Chu. At its peak in the 1980s, the company chalked up annual revenues of US $3 billion and employed over 33,000 people. A sad demise came in August 1992 when the company filed for bankruptcy protection. While multiple reasons could be attributed to the failure, one top reason argued by most critics is that the company was incapable of keeping in pace with the change of technology and market. Staying in the old rut, the company had been too slow to respond to the growth of personal computers and was unable to compete against major rivals like IBM. Besides, even if there were some change efforts, they were unsuccessful because detailed work of planning and implementing to ensure what actually would take place in the real world was not seen (Edgelow, 2012). In the end, sales of personal computers soared and they quickly took market share from Wang's word-processors and its more expensive mid-sized computers. What customers wanted was not responsively catered leading to demand perpetually being shifted away.

On the other hand, the case of Hong Kong Ocean Park shows how a company could turn the table with rapid change. Ocean Park Hong Kong, commonly known as Ocean Park, is a marine animal theme park and amusement park founded in 1977. Before Hong Kong Disneyland opened to visitors in 2005, Ocean Park was the only remaining theme park in Hong Kong struggled on whilst at death's door. Lacklustre shows, antiquated attractions, and a mildew environment discouraged attendance causing a net loss of HK $4.1 million in 2003. In 2004, Allan Zeman GBM, GBS, JP was invited by the then-Chief Executive of Hong Kong, Tung Chee-hwa, to become the chairman of Ocean Park. Zeman believed that the marine park's potential was far from being fully explored and niche had to be redefined. Upon drastic change of the park's image and marketing strategies, Zeman managed to raise visitor numbers despite the opening of rival Hong Kong Disneyland, making the park more attractive and, remarkably, generated record profits just the next year. In 2007 Forbes referred Zeman as 'Hong Kong's Mouse Killer' because of the success that Ocean Park is having while Hong Kong Disneyland struggles. During the financial year ended June 2011, the park generated an income of HK $1.2 billion with a net profit of HK $105.1 million.

In contrast, there are examples of rapid change which had

disaster written all over. During the 1997 policy address on October, 1997, the former HKSAR chief executive Mr. Tung Chee-hwa announced his infamous housing plan of producing at least 85,000 housing flats per year for ten years. The intention was to tackle the high rising property prices in Hong Kong so that it would be easier for people to own property. Within a year upon introduction of the policy, housing price in Hong Kong dropped more than half, adding hail to snow by the Asian financial crisis. The housing price collapsed further and housing developers had a lot of troubles selling their flats. Such fall in the housing market caused many home owners to be 'negative asset' holders as their properties fell below the purchase prices while they had to pay mortgage. By 2003, Hong Kong housing market hit bottom with a shred of value by 70%. In July 2003, prompted by dissatisfaction against the Hong Kong Government and blunders by the Tung Chee-hwa administration, a mass protest of 500,000 marchers broke out. The protest was the largest seen in Hong Kong since the 1997 handover. Eventually the housing policy disappeared into thin air.

Another example where pain permeates before any merits is the hot topic of Moral, Civic and National Education, a newly developed curricular to be implemented in all Hong Kong primary and secondary schools starting September 2012. According to the Hong Kong Education Bureau (EDB), the curricular aims at "fostering students' positive values and attitudes through the school curriculum and the provision of diversified learning experiences." Nonetheless, the curricular has drawn huge resistance and doubt from stakeholders because they are convinced that it is a form of 'political brainwash'. In fact, public were shocked that policy makers had use taxpayers' money to fund the production of teaching materials which are politically biased filled as well with highly prejudicial opinion. In July 2012, at least 90,000 parents marched on the street with their children under the blazing sun opposing the launch of the curricular.

Student and teacher strikes are brewing underway in many local schools should the government insist on launching the curricular in September. The latest development is, Scholarism Hong Kong, a well-known and sympathised student body formed by secondary school students, has camped outside the government headquarters in Central since August 31st, 2012. Some even on hunger strike simultaneously, calling it 'occupying HK government', to protest against the curricular.

The above two cases demonstrate how an organisation won't turn up trumps just by having 'good intentions'. Providing that the two cases did inflict big impact on public, adopting rapid change plans as such were simply foolish and doomed to fail because, firstly, the magnitude of impact was hastily measured if not totally unmeasured, and secondly, the fundamental drive cum reactions of stakeholders were incautiously undermined if not totally ignored. Besides, policy makers of the above two cases seemingly showed no flexibility and sensibility in execution leading to be big flops. The ultimate tragedy was that there was no damage control whatsoever of the negative results incurred. Further, while organizations going through major change should ensure their people gain a positive experience of the process (Neal, 2008), stakeholders in the above two cases were either left to suffer or because a burnt child dreads the fire; further persuasion effort of the change plan would be made almost impossible. Should there be a second chance, assuming that these change plans are justifiable, it is more advisable that they are carried out incrementally with high quality management and leadership. Ideally, policy makers could have taken the resistance as a form of feedback and administer effective conversation that gives the change effort a higher profile while establishing good rapport (Ford and Ford, 2009). The important lesson is that when deciding which type of change is appropriate, it is vital for management to consider a wide range of factors like the magnitude, pace, timing and other variables of the change plan with kid gloves in order to maximize the benefits and effects.

Furthermore, even when an organisation has successfully implemented a change plan, rapid or not, it does not mean work is done once and for all. Going back to the case of Ocean Park Hong Kong, with peak season flow of visitors in 2012, Ocean Park was accused in August 2012 for 'significantly increasing the work load' of dolphins. Denying the accusation, Ocean Park said the dolphin shows would enhance public's concern of marine life and promote wildlife conservation. The park explained that the dolphins would get adequate rest and play before each show. At the same time, Zeman felt insulted and angry about the accusation because he believed that these shows contained educational and conservation messages rather than being just circus shows. The accusation has drawn much attention of public, and discussion has arisen for whether or not animals should go through 'servitude' for profit making. A group of animal rights activists has launched an on-line joint petition to condemn Ocean Park. In March 2012, Ric O'Barry who starred in Oscar best documentary winner "The Cove" had already had a debate with Zeman as to whether the park was distorting the natural behaviour of dolphins, making them depressed and even suicidal. The Hong Kong Dolphin Conservation Society questions the practice of Ocean Park, saying dolphins have no choice but to perform whenever they are instructed to.

In this light, management of Ocean Park may want to note, first, the cost for Ocean Park's corrective actions and damage to the company's image is yet to be fully understood. Second, even if the issue of dolphins is temporarily solved, it does not mean other marine life like sea lion or other animals are exempted. Third, while many EU countries, including Cyprus and the United Kingdom have prohibited marine animal shows or captivation of dolphins, it is doubtful whether Hong Kong can stand alone in the long run. Fourth, in terms of damage control and regaining market confidence, challenge facing management lies in how to prevent ill-structured problems and ignorance with respect to alternatives and consequences, and make partial search for solutions based on biased evaluation, selection and monitoring alternatives (Heracleous, 1994). All these together are things up to Zeman to think about, but the immediate morals are, first, unwanted cost is inevitable should a company become complacent. Second, since people's intention is always to be anticipated behind resistance and understanding such intention substantiates change of people, teams, organisations, communities and even countries in desired ways (Boyatzis, 2006), it is worth therefore for an organisation to open up sincere communication with stakeholders and understand what they truly concern. Ultimately, cost is to be minimized by continual improvement and sensibility towards the pulse and needs of stakeholders.

In conclusion, globalization of business environment today entails an inclination towards rapid and continuous change of organisations. While continuous change is definite, there are times when rapid change is not recommended particularly when the pain from resistance exceeds far more than what the plan aims to gain. It is therefore critical for management to consider a wide range of factors before determining which type of plan is suitable. Even when rapid change is necessary, management is advised to always keep abreast of the needs and sentiments of stakeholders. At last, no change plan is sustainable forever because no environment is permanent. Management of an organisation therefore should commit to continual improvement and incorporate an ever-changing corporate culture so that any change plan would come at ease.

References

Abrahamson, E. (2000). Change without Pain. *Harvard Business Review Vol. 78 Issue 4, 75-79*

Boyatzis, R. E. (2006). An overview of intentional change from a complexity perspective. *Journal of Management Development, Vol.25 No.7, 607-623.*

Cokins, C. (2010). *Why Do Once Successful Companies Fail?* Posted March 17, 2010 SmartData Collective http://www.smartdatacollective.com/Home/25543

Dunphy D. & Stace D., (1993). *The Strategic Management of Corporate Change.* London: Tavistock Institute

Edgelow, C. (2012). Who is in charge of change? *Industrial and Commercial Training, Vol. 44, Issue 1, 3-8*

Ford, E.D., & Ford, L.W. (2009) Managing Yourself, Decoding Resistance to Change Strong leaders can hear and learn from their critics. *Harvard business review, Apr., 99-103*

Heracleous, L. Th. (1994). Rational Decision Making: Myth or Reality? *Management Development Review, Vol. 7 Issue 4, 16-23*

Howell, J.P., & and Paris, L (2000). Leadership for strategic change. *Leadership & organization development journal, Vol. 21, no. 3, 150-156*

Lee, K. V., (1994) *Wang Laboratories Inc : a case study of strategic and organizational success and failure.* Hong Kong: University of Hong Kong

Marković, M. (2008) Managing The Organizational Change and Culture In The Age of Globalization. *Journal of Business Economics and Management Vol. 9, no. 1, 3-11*

Neal, A. (2008). Preparing the organization for change. *Strategic HR Review, Vol.7 No.6, 30-35.*

Want, J. H. (1993) Managing radical change. *Journal of business strategy, Vol. 14, No. 3, 20-28*
Learn More: Former CE Tung Chee-hwa's Housing Policy
Ming Pao Daily News – 2010/04/28

Moral, Civic and National Education. Hong Kong Government Site. Retrieved on August 19, 2012:
http://www.edb.gov.hk/index.aspx?nodeID=2397&langno=1

Spectrum of debate on moral and national education in Hong Kong
gb times. Retrieved on August 19, 2012:
http://www.gbtimes.com/lifestyle/social-issues/spectrum-debate-moral-and-national-education-hong-kong

Hong Kong Ocean Park web site homepage. Retrieved on August 19, 2012: http://www.oceanpark.com.hk/html/en/home/

Hong Kong Dolphin Conservation Society homepage:
http://www.hkdcs.org/

海豚表演討好觀眾　牠真的快樂嗎？Economic Daily News - 2012/08/14

海洋公園海豚恢復日演四場　Sing Tao Daily – 2012年8月18日

稱視動物為子女　僅為應暑期人流加騷　　　Apple Daily -

2012年8月18日
拒認虐待　海洋公園：海豚自願

海豚「加班」惹批評 海洋公園稱有休息 *Ming Pao Daily News*
2012/08/13

盛智文：香港海洋公園加價保營運吸游客2009年07月28日09:0
4 來源：中國新聞網 Retrieved on August 19, 2012:
http://hm.people.com.cn/BIG5/42276/9734163.html

心在香港 TVB Programme -盛智文.　Retrieved on August 20,
2012:
http://www.youtube.com/watch?v=6z6fTrpl_h8

Sunday Taipan, now TV progamme, guest Allan Zeman (Starting at
8:00). Retrieved on August 20, 2012:
http://www.tudou.com/programs/view/mUDe9BxOshI/

盛智文又扮鬼Sina News HK 2009-08-14, Retrieved on August 21,
2012:
http://news.sina.com.hk/cgi-
bin/nw/show.cgi/2/1/1/1231546/1.html

談管理 喜歡當「巴士司機」 *Ming Pao Daily News* 2007/6/15
Retrieved on August 21, 2012:
http://ol.mingpao.com/cfm/style5.cfm?File=20070615/sta12/yia2
.txt

Nothing is impossible—聽盛智文博士講座有感. Personal Blog of
：卓友森2009-12-19 14:13:00　Retrieved on August 21, 2012:
http://blog.meadin.com/u1/cheukyousen/20091219141355.html

Strategic Management in a Rapidly Changing World

Change your thoughts and you change your world.
— Norman Vincent Peale

Globalization overseeing the modern business world suggests that "change" is the only thing that remains constant. In a time when business is conducted with less boundaries and competition cultivated by collaborating across time, distance and culture (Marković, 2008), a fundamental shift in the organisational culture are mandatory for sustaining competiveness, longevity and prosperity. In dealing with fierce and volatile changing forces, CEO of organisations inevitably have to go about change management with well-defined strategic thinking, choice and position.

This present paper aims to articulate the relationship between rapid change and strategic management. The paper begins by outlining the concept of rapid change and how it fits within transformational change and strategic management. Next, the paper discusses the various models and theories used to assess rapid change and the way CEO should respond. Finally, the paper evaluates two examples and concludes that change management is necessary yet it takes prudence and sensitivity to sustain.

Rapid, volatile, discontinuous change in a globalized environment can be summarized as follows: First, rapid technological change and advancement is prevalent. Second, the size of investments required for global business can be enormous. Third, the post global financial crisis business environment is more turbulent and dangerous before. Fourth, hyper-competition is escalating where competitive advantage has become significantly harder to sustain across not just one or two industries, but a broad range of industries (Wiggins & Ruefli, 2005).In this light,the cliché of "manages today from tomorrow" with rapid organisational change is predominant for any company to survive. Rapid organisational change, or 'transformational change', involves drastically and dramatically reshaping the competitive capabilities of the organisation (Want, 1993).This is painful because people are habitual and old routines which give them a sense of security. But time waits for nobody and the consequences of not complying with external volatility can be disastrous. The alternative, of course, is 'incremental change' which emphasizes more on melting the ice-cube incrementally. While opinion diverges as to which way is the best, the question for management remains to be how to strategically balance the necessary change initiatives so that above average results are achieved not just in the present fluctuating moment, but are sustainable in the long-run.

With respect to the rapidly changing business environment, Dunphy and Stace (1993) argue that organizational development is better represented by transformational change with a directive leadership style. Landrum, Howell, and Paris (2000) echo the idea by describing how great leaders of modern organizations are expected to have the core competence of communicating a vision and mobilizing the energy necessary for rapid change actions. These studies demonstrate that an effective leadership style is crucial in motivating the necessary organisational change. The ideal scenario comes when the internal environment moves forward in a way such that it outraces the rapid changes of the external environment: When management has the foresight to change ahead of the rampant currents from all directions. Such endeavour should certainly entail precise planning, implementation and evaluation of the multidimensionalstrategic management process.

When chaos emerges and wakeup calls are knocking on the door, old state and mind-set are threaten to engage in a position to shift. At this stage of critical period, the company would either pass through the 'bottle-neck' and survive, or simply perish. However, as mentioned, with strategic management which incorporate vision and a commitment to constant monitoring of the changing environment, it is certainly much more preferable to take preventive actions rather than their corrective counterparts. As Piderit (2000) proposes, the importance of examining the evolution of employee responses to change from a bottom-up, egalitarian approach should be highlighted. Such preventive actions are conducted via the strategic management dimension which comprises effective process, content and context. At the very minimum, the organisation should be committed to maintain a dynamic stability of the organisation by reconfiguring existing practices and business models (Abrahamson, 2000). In short, the cost for a company to stay complacent is most likely to be unaffordable in an era where uncertainty and unpredictability prevail.

When carrying out change management, the CEO would never underestimate the resistance from stakeholders and pressures from the environment as the 'lovely' status quo has been disturbed which is upsetting if not intimidating. Though, with the CEO's commitment in continuous improvement, prior to deciding where to draw the fine line in the spectrum of change, transformational or transitional, the CEO would consider a wide range of factors like the magnitude, pace and timing with kid gloves in order to minimize pain and maximize the benefits. Considering people's intention sticks closely behind resistance and understanding such intention substantiates change management in desired ways (Boyatzis, 2006), it is therefore equally important or the CEO to open up sincere communication with stakeholders in understanding their needs and concerns.

The classic case of Wang Laboratories illustrates what could happen to a company staying in the old rut. Wang Laboratories chalked up annual revenue of US $3 billion during its peak in the 1980's but eventually filed bankruptcy in 1992. Many reasons may have been attributed to the failure, but one top reason was that the company was incapable of keeping in pace with the change in technology and customer needs. The company failed to respond to the growth of PC and was losing market shares to major rivals like IBM. While the sales of PC soared, customers simply walked away from the obsolete Wang's word-processors. In contrast, the case of Hong Kong Ocean Park shows how a company could turn the table around with prompt actions. The Park used to be wandering in front of death's door with lacklustre shows and poor attractions. The mildew environment of the park also discouraged attendance and caused consecutive net loss. To survive, Allan Zeman was invited as the new CEO in 2004. Upon drastic change of the park's image and marketing niche, for example, giving the park with a "refreshed" new look with "rejuvenated" attitude of the staff, purchasing new marine life and rides for amusement park, and putting on new shows and themes, Zeman successfully raised visitor numbers despite Hong Kong Disneyland opened to visitors in 2005. In 2007, Forbes referred Zeman as 'Hog Kong's Mouse Killer' because of the success that Ocean Park enjoyed while Disneyland struggled.

In conclusion, a globalized business environment encourages a strategic inclination towards transformational change. While rapid change, internal or external, has become more and more a natural phenomenon nowadays, the job of the CEO is to manoeuvre the change plan with prudence and sensitivity. In addition, the key to strategic management of rapid change is to consider a variety of factors and have open communication channels with stakeholders in understanding their sentiments and needs. Finally, no plan of change is perpetual as the environment is not going to be permanent. Therefore, the management of an organization should be committed to continuous improvement and incorporate a changing corporate culture; any change plan is accommodated with optimal collection of unique resources and capabilities, thus increasing the likelihood of long-term success.

References

Abrahamson, E. (2000). Change without Pain. *Harvard Business Review Vol. 78 Issue 4, 75-79*

Boyatzis, R. E. (2006). An overview of intentional change from a complexity perspective. *Journal of Management Development, Vol.25 No.7, 607-623.*

Dunphy D. &Stace D., (1993).*The Strategic Management of Corporate Change.* London: Tavistock Institute

Landrum, N. E., Howell, J. P., & Paris, L. (2000).Leadership for strategic change. *Leadership & Organization Development Journal, 21*(3), 150-156.

Marković, M. (2008) Managing The Organizational Change and Cultureln The Age of Globalization. *Journal of Business Economics and Management Vol. 9, no. 1, 3-11*

Piderit, S. K. (2000). Rethinking resistance and recognizing ambivalence: A multidimensional view of attitudes toward an organizational change. *Academy of management review, 25*(4), 783-794.

Want, J. H. (1993) Managing radical change. *Journal of business strategy, Vol. 14, No. 3, 20-28*

Wiggins, R. R., &Ruefli, T. W. (2005). Schumpeter's ghost: Is hypercompetition making the best of times shorter? *Strategic Management Journal, 26*(10), 887-911.

The Future of Relationship Marketing

Marketing is too important to be left to the marketing department.

-David Packard

Since the time Relationship Marketing (RM) emerged as a popular new paradigm in the 1980's, it has been a focus at the forefront of services marketing practice and academic research. While a shift of focus from customer acquisition to customer retention has been observed, the maturity of services marketing which emphasized on quality, increased recognition of RM benefits for both the company and the customer, cum technological advances all contribute further RM's development. Yet, there is also a debate about the relevance of RM within markets that are changing very quickly. Is relationship marketing a passing fashion that can be ignored by business? Is it relevant for all businesses? Is this relevancy expected to become more important in the future?

Before going further to answering these questions, it is obviously worthwhile to examine the definition of RM. One of the most cited and most 'elegant and succinct' (Egan, 2011) definition is from Grönroos (1994):

> "RM is to identify and establish, maintain and enhance and when necessary also to terminate relationships with customers and other

stakeholder, at a profit, so that the objectives of all parties are met, and that this is done by a mutual exchange and fulfilment of promise."

Parvatiyar (2001) defines RM as a marketing paradigm which attracts, maintains and enhances customer relationships. In the context of modern business environment, companies have few reasons to completely neglect the impact of RM. Inasmuch of a more globalized and turbulent market environment; customers are not consistently the same 'good customers' anymore. As Sheth & Parvatiyar (1995) argues, it is necessary for marketers to understand what motivates consumers when developing a theory of RM which encourages the consumer to patronize the same marketer in subsequent choice while maintaining psychological comfort. The advantages of RM commonly identified by research include, first, because loyal customers generate more revenue, a company's long term profits are more guaranteed by investing on building customer's retention and loyalty. Besides, the costs to maintain existing customers are lower than acquiring new customers. Hence, by reducing marketing costs, RM has also the potential to increase marketing effectiveness and efficiency. Finally, established 'relationships' would also serve as an important source of substantial competitive advantage, in contrast of traditional transactional marketing (TM) where product features, benefits and promotions are of heavier weights. RM has therefore been compared as the two ends of a spectrum and a marketing paradigm shift from transactional to relationship marketing has been proposed.

On the other hand, since RM is by nature a target and culture specific marketing practice, it is certainly not relevant to all businesses. A common reason why RM is not relevant to all businesses, or at least not a priority for them, is that these businesses have valid reasons to incline more heavily on the traditional marketing approach (TMA). To these businesses, TMA is sufficient for maximizing profit; projects like increasing customers' switching cost or building switching barriers do not really matter to them. There are no significant incentives to these businesses to engage in more than necessary relationship building activities. For instance, a McDonald fan may keep going for a Big Mac every day for the next twenty years, but building relationship overtly with him/her does not mean a whole lot to the company. In short, these businesses tend to rely more on traditional marketing mix or the four 'P's: Price, Product, Place, Promotion, and efforts on building relationship is observed, yet placed in a periphery position and served more as an auxiliary scheme. The case gets more obvious when it comes to companies serving the basic needs of customers and product differentiation is relatively small in the market. No matter how these companies tilt their orientations for adapting change, their focuses are shed within a confine mixed with production, sales, and a relatively small bag of tricks used for market manipulation.

While RM is unlikely to be a passing fashion as discussed, the succeeding question is whether or not RM is expected to be more important in future? To answer this question, we will have to first take a closer look at how modern market and consumers behave. Markets come to terms that the good old days of buying and selling is gone. Compared to the needs of modern consumers, consumers were more easily satisfied in the old days when sales of products were more orientated to an environment which were more stable and less information and technology. It was natural and normal for the company to consider economies of scale being a core focus of the business because that would mean a maximization of profits and efficient operation. As long as the company managed to promote its sales in quantity and cost advantages were obtained due to expansion, a company would considered to be doing fine.

In contrast, modern markets are more complex and turbulent due to a globalization and advance of technology. Individuals are bestowed with more power and presented with a vast range of information sources where they are apt to 'rebel' as they ever did before. Individuals are fully aware of the existence of more variety of brands in any given product category, however, it would be impossible for them to consider all brands for purchase. Individuals are more selective, sensitive, critical and demanding towards the choices they are presented with. In terms of Porter's framework of industrial analysis (Peng, 2009), while competition among rivalries are greater these days, the bargaining power of buyers are substantially stronger as well. At the same time, the threats from entrants and substitute products are more unbearable than ever. Most marketing efforts which did work before should fail miserably at present because a company cannot simply just brag about the features and benefits of a product and expect good sales right the way. While attention and awareness of a product is achieved with reasonable efforts, consumers do not necessary need to 'feel right' about a product or the company amongst all the alternatives, which means credibility is never attained. Getting consumers to take your brand seriously is far harder than making them aware that the brand exists. Therefore, a consumer has to first take the brand seriously, that the brand is credible, before proceed further to make up a consideration set which measures such credibility for his or her purchase decision. A consumer may not be taking your brand seriously either because they are not fully aware of your marketing mix or because there are some serious misperceptions. Entering consumer consideration sets requires a careful understanding of the marketplace. Throwing money on advertising and commercials, will, typically, not solve this problem.

This reinforces the concept where RM should continue to have a sustainable position in contemporary and businesses should have the versatility of juggling between the TM and RM. Nonetheless, since change is the only thing being unchanged in today's business environment, in order to best satisfy consumer wants and sustain relationship building efforts, marketers are is expected to be heads up on the pressure and forces raging from all directions and take the necessary measures for change. In light of what factors are likely to reshape the future direction of RM, various theories have been proposed. Palmatier (2008) outlines the future of RM to include the followings: First, research on RM should be more focused on customer's benefits and costs instead of just the seller's. Next, efforts could be made in understanding the impact of RM on knowledge acquisition and innovation. Berry (1995) believes that although RM is developing, it has not reached maturity because there are "a baker's dozen of researchable questions", for example, "what service characteristics increase or decrease the appeal of RM to customers?" which help sketch RM future directions. Sheth (2002) suggests that the paradigm of RM is likely to shift once again into customer relationship marketing (CRM) which covers a conceptually broader phenomenon of business activity. Yet, Parvatiyar & Sheth (2001) have to admit that whether CRM or RM will become "a well-respected, freestanding, and distinct discipline in marketing" remains to be an important question for scholars to find out.

The problems with the above theories are that either they may have a certain degree of difficulty of agreeing internally or they may have confounded the causes and consequences of the establishment of a discipline. It goes without saying that the antecedents for a future depends on what happened in the past and what is happening in the present. When more data are available then it is certainly the case that the description of the future will be more accurate. Looking back at the scenario of modern market, we can see that technology allows businesses to target the specifications of a product to a smaller and smaller group of people. The recent cases of technology giants Sony and Panasonic being recently downgraded on their debt ratings to "junk" status suggest that not only businesses should commit to continual improvement and incorporate an ever-changing corporate culture to meet the challenges from all directions, but they have far better competitive advantages if greater product differentiation is achieved. Unlike their rivalries Samsung or LG, Sony and Panasonic are not ready to make products which are manifested with a more personal touch. As discussed, despite that fact that product differentiation is sufficient and salient for long term prosperity of sales, its nature is transactional which means long term profits are not guaranteed.

In this regard, can we possibly combine product differentiation and RM as possible future direction of RM? Considering the resources available for modern business culture and with the right technology, companies can make the personal product that satisfies smaller and more specific cohort of consumers. The hybrid of production and consumption has in fact merged into a new marketing term called 'prosuming'. The most interesting and enchanting element about prosuming and mass customization is that not only has it provided a platform for product differentiation, it also has provided a new way of establishing relationship between the customer and the company. The dynamics is based on the very fact that because customers have a hand in the creation of the product they are more likely to be satisfied with the final result. While customers are being kept in stitches, they have taught the company how to please them, and the company now has a customer with a much fuller relationship with them than before. Customer relationship starts with creating a product which has 'a niche of one' and modern technologies should help escalate and transform the levels of relationships available to customers.

The potential for allowing customers to gain new experience in the consumption process is a step further to CRM. The reason CRM practices is still far short of ideal is that while money is spent on people and product, there is no way to control individual negative sentiments or discontentment. Because how could you do anything do please anyone? While people have been talking about providing value for customers so as to increase sales, the efforts behind are so easily fallen in void because they rely too much on assumption and customers' perception are way too difficult to grasp. As Ravald & Grönroos (1996) mention, the concept of providing value has evident risk as it is used without any efforts and commitments to understand the underlying meanings. Ravald & Grönroos (1996) further mention that a successful way of providing value could be orientated on customer's experience as to reduce the customer-perceived sacrifice by minimizing the relationship costs for the customer. The lost cost is achievable when businesses get less involved in deliberate effort, but more advisable to go ahead and let the customers define on their own what they value , creates and shapes on their own, an experience that reinforces their inner desires while mutually sharable with others. As Winter (2001) notes, the notion of customer satisfaction is expanded to change CRM to Customer Experience Management (CEM). According to Winter (2001), the idea behind CEM is that it is more critical than ever for marketers to measure customer's reactions to contacts made and develop immediate responses to negative experiences. As customers experience grows, size of consideration sets increase at both the brand and category levels (Johnson and Lehmann, 1997).

To illustrate the above principles, let's take a look at Apple Corporation (APPLE). First, iTunes is provided by the company as free software as well as a jukebox of customers' own music. Because iTunes is free, APPLE has to put forth extra investment to maintain this 'extra benefit' as perceived by APPLE the customer. Reciprocally, nonetheless, APPLE gets to know more about the customer via regular contacts and thus able to create higher switching costs for the customer when considering an alternative platform or operational system (OS). Next, customers get helpful tips and suggestions on issues like 'how to get started', 'accessories to buy', or 'upgrade notifications' via emails ever since their first purchase of APPLE product. These extra services, as perceived by customers, show that APPLE 'cares' about their after-sale experience and in turns means APPLE 'cares' about them. Moreover, rival hardware manufacturers are not as ready and willing to update their software products so frequently and passionately. They are primarily interested in selling new hardware. APPLE, on the other hand, is quite happy to lose out on some hardware upgrades so as to keep people within their 'ecosystem'. Finally, APPLE is highly selective and deliberate in hiring staff with expertise in the products in order to provide a much higher level of sales experience and support inn their many retail shops compared to rival companies. In contrast, rival companies tend not to have their own retail shops and they depend more on other retailers for similar kind of engagement. All of the above explains why there are so many so-called 'APPLE fan boys' who have intense loyalty to the company and will buy its products almost regardless of the quality or specifications of competing products.

In conclusion, while RM is an on-going field of study, there is evidence that it can be combined with factors like product differentiation and CRM. Arising from the analysis made above, with respect to possible future of RM, the key recommendations are:

1. That a company does not just develop RM based on assumptions: The disadvantages of depending heavily on assumptions are, first, it takes too many resources to establish the assumptions, and second, once they are formed, they are in position to be justified which means slow in reaction to change.
2. A platform for consumers to manifest their needs and sentiments is delicately created, which follows naturally then,

the company invests in maintaining genuine versatility for necessary refinement and update of such platform.

3. When manifestation of consumers' needs and sentiments are expressed and communicated via their experience on using the products and inevitably being involved in producing, tailor making, customizing, modifying the product being purchased.

4. Such paradigm of exchange between the company and consumers, i.e., the company creates an experience platform for consumers, and the consumers' needs being catered by such platform, and proceed with mutual reinforcement of the paradigm not only enhance loyalty between the two but long term mutual benefits.

References

Berry, L. L. (1995). Relationship marketing of services—growing interest, emerging perspectives. *Journal of the Academy of marketing science*, 23(4), 236-245.

Egan, John (2011), *Relationship Marketing: Exploring Relational Strategies in Marketing (4th ed.)*, Prentice Hall, England.

Johnson, M. D., & Lehmann, D. R. (1997). Consumer experience and consideration sets for brands and product categories. *Advances in consumer research*, 24, 295-300.

MacInnis, D. J., & Price, L. L. (1990). An exploratory study of the effects of imagery processing and consumer experience on expectations and satisfaction. *Advances in consumer research*, 17(1), 41-47.

Palmatier, R. W. (2008). *Relationship marketing*. Cambridge, MA: Marketing Science Institute.

Parvatiyar, A., & Sheth, J. N. (2001). Customer relationship management: emerging practice, process, and discipline. *Journal of Economic and Social Research*, 3(2), 1-34.

Peng, Mike W. (2009). Global *Strategic Management, 2nd Edition.* South-Western – CENGAGE Learning

Ravald, A., & Grönroos, C. (1996). The value concept and relationship marketing. *European journal of marketing*, 30(2), 19-30.

Sheth, J. N. (2002). The future of relationship marketing. *Journal of Services Marketing*, 16(7), 590-592.

Sheth, J. N., & Parvatiyar, A. (1995). Relationship marketing in consumer markets: antecedents and consequences. *Journal of the Academy of marketing Science*, 23(4), 255-271.

Winer, R. S. (2001). *Customer relationship management: a framework, research directions, and the future.* Haas School of Business.

Supply Chain Flexibility

So what if all those chains were suddenly cut, how would you make something? How would you keep people alive? And that was something I wanted to explore.

-Max Brooks

In today's globalized business environment, markets are becoming more dynamic and customer-driven. Competiveness increases as customers are demanding better quality and service along with expectations on higher reliability and faster delivery. New product innovations and improvements in manufacturing processes are essential as technological developments are occurring at a much faster pace. As all the domains in a business strive for change in order to secure long term success, the supply chain are in a particularly critical position to go through continuous evolution.

As we understand, the supply chain encompasses a flow of products and services from raw materials manufacturers, intermediate products manufacturers, end product manufacturers, wholesalers and distributors and retailers. Effective supply chain management (SCM) is to be carried out in a way such that suppliers, manufacturers, warehouses, and stores are efficiently integrated, and at the end merchandise is produced and distributed in the right quantities, to the right locations and at the right time with minimal total system cost (Simchi-Levi et al., 2009). In short, without effective SCM, problem such as conflicting goals and objectives may occur. Inasmuch the supply chain consists of various partners and organizations, the supply chain is a natural breeding ground for conflict.

Specific and measurable solutions thus need to be explored and developed in order to align those goals and objectives, extending to inventory control, operation efficiency, total cost reduction, lead time and logistics enhancement so forth. Supply chain flexibility (SCF) is therefore suggested to be one key factor in dealing with these problems. Flexibility may be defined as the ability to adapt, change or react as you like with insignificant penalty in time, effort, cost or performance. In regard to modern business environment, as diversity and uncertainty inevitably increases, companies are choosing to respond by adding flexibility as a dimension to their operation strategies. Flexibility can improve the company's competitiveness, particularly for the decision-making process of implementing technologies. Nevertheless, managers do not necessarily have a thorough understanding of flexibility because focus is more conventionally placed on the 'obvious' aspect like machine flexibility than on total system flexibility. Focusing flexibility on the implementation of technology, unfortunately, does not necessarily lead to enhanced competitiveness. Besides, even though there has been a tremendous amount of research on the landscape of operation flexibility, most scope has been confined to intra-firm flexibility which does not extend beyond the firm (Duclos *et al.*, 2003). In this case, interactions among firms as well as firm to environment are not adequately dealt with, which should affect the overall design of effective supply chain strategies. After all, the real competition is supply chain-to-supply chain, not firm-to-firm (Grigore, 2007). Finally, much of the existing research also has a limited definition of SCF and describes it simply as a reactive means to cope with diversity and uncertainty (Stevenson and Spring, 2007). Possibilities of enhancing the validity of the concept, such as resolving supply chain conflicts and other issues mentioned earlier in this paper could have been more explored. Therefore, the objectives of this paper are to, i., explore the meaning of flexibility in a supply chain context and the definitions of key concepts by reviewing a selection of existing literature, ii., attempt to generate a list of potential research questions with respect to the concept of supply chain flexibility, and iii., propose possible direction towards evaluating and measuring supply chain performance in relation with SCF.

In the paper titled "Supply chain flexibility", Grigore (2007) describes the features of SCF with respect to a proliferation of papers:
1. Deals with product development, manufacturing logistics, and spanning flexibilities.
2. Improves a company's efficiency, simultaneously serves as a significant measure of supply chain performance.
3. Encompasses flexibility dimensions that directly impact a firm's customers and are the shared responsibility of two or more functions along the supply chain, whether internal (marketing, manufacturing) or external (suppliers, channel members) to the firm.

Based primarily on the model developed by Duclos *et at.* (2003) and Vickery*et al.* (1999), Girgore (2007) provides an overview on SCF components and dimensions: The components of SCF are abilities of being flexible whereas the dimensions are qualities of a firm being flexible in a supply chain. This model as a matter of fact has been a popular topic for discussion in the field of supply chain management since introduction. The model of SCF is summarized in the following two tables:

Supply Chain Flexibility Components

	Components	Definitions
1	Operations system flexibility	The ability to configure assets and operations
2	Market flexibility	The ability to mass customize and build close relationships with customers

3	Logistics flexibility	The ability to cost effectively receive and deliver product
4	Supply flexibility	The ability to reconfigure the supply chain
5	Organizational flexibility	The ability to align labor force skills to the needs of the supply chain
6	Information systems flexibility	The ability to align information system architectures and systems

Supply Chain Flexibility Dimensions:

	Components	Definitions
a	Product flexibility	the ability to handle difficult, non-standard orders, to meet special customer specifications, and to produce
b	Volume flexibility	the ability to effectively increase or decrease aggregate production in response to customer demand).
c	Routing flexibility	the capability of processing a part through varying routes by using alternative machines, flexible material handling, and flexible transporting network
d	Delivery flexibility	the company's ability to adapt lead times to the customer requirement
e	Trans-shipment flexibility	movement of stock between locations at the same echelon level
f	Postponement	the ability of keeping products in

	flexibility	their generic form as long as possible
g	Sourcing flexibility	the company's ability to find another supplier for each specific component or raw material
h	Responsiveness	the company's ability to respond to the needs of its target markets
i	Launch flexibility	the ability to rapidly introduce many new products and product varieties
j	Access flexibility	the ability to provide widespread or intensive distribution coverage

Sánchez & Pérez (2005) provide in-depth analysis and interpretation on the above model. Following the work of Duclos et al. (2003) and Vickery et al. (1999), Sánchez & Pérez (2005) develop a framework of supply chain flexibility dimensions that includes both process flexibility and logistics flexibility. Such elaboration, being a conceptual model, describes the fact that this is a hierocratic classification of flexibility where:

a. The first three flexibility dimensions (Product, Volume and Routing) are 'shop -floor' capabilities that impact on supply chain (basic flexibility).

b. The following three dimensions (delivery, Transshipment and Postponement) are one level up, located at company level (system flexibility).

c. The top four flexibility dimensions (Launch, Sourcing, Response and Access) are linked to the customer-supplier relationships in the supply chain (aggregate flexibility).

In terms of analyzing the fundamentals of SCF, Sánchez & Pérez (2005) suggest that the supply chain components and their inter-relationships should be looked at in order to evaluate their impact. In this light, Sánchez & Pérez (2005) propose two main aspects:

i. Process flexibility of each supply chain plant, concerning the number of product, &
ii. Logistics flexibility, related to the different logistics strategies which can be adopted either to release a product to a market or to procure a component from a supplier.

Sánchez & Pérez (2005) further suggest that there is a positive relation between a superior performance in flexibility capabilities and firm. They also discover that aggregate flexibility capabilities are more positively related to firm performance than basic flexibility capabilities. Finally, it is indicated in the paper that with higher environmental uncertainty, technological complexity and mutual understanding, flexibility capabilities are enhanced in supply chains, but with lower interdependence among the agents involved in the supply chain.

Examining each of these dimensions in details, Calantone and Dröge (2006) argue that volume flexibility and launch flexibility are key responses to marketing practices uncertainty and product uncertainty. Calantone and Dröge (2006) recommend viewing flexibility from the perspective of the entire value-adding system, i.e., total system flexibility which implies that SCF should be examined from an integrative, customer-oriented perspective. Thus, SCF should encompass those flexibilities that directly add value in the customer's eyes and are the shared responsibility of two or more functions along the supply chain. Furthermore, Calantone and Dröge (2006) believe that SCF are rewarded most effectively when supply chain management could enhance competitive performance by closely integrating the internal functions within a firm and linking them with the external operations of suppliers and channel members.

While Calantone & Dröge (2006) attempt to describe the relationship between flexibility and supply chain management, Prater et al (2001)describe flexibility to be an extension of 'agility' which instigate more insight towards the concept of SCF. In the paper 'International supply chain agility', Prater et al (2001) see the supply chain as a combination of sourcing, manufacturing and delivery. The term 'supply chain agility' is introduced in the paper where joining supply chain flexibility and supply chain speed. According to Prater et al (2001), firms must respond to changes quickly in a useful time frame. Nevertheless, measures taken to increase agility often lead to increases in complexity, which works against agility. Thus, Prater et al (2001) propose a theoretical construct linking elements of uncertainty with aspects of agility, pointing out the two-edged nature of the requisite capabilities. According to Prater et al (2001), flexibility may be broken down into two capabilities: (1) the promptness with; and (2) the degree to which a firm can adjust its supply chain speed, destinations, and volumes. It is further argued that if a deficiency was serious enough to limit supply chain agility, the firm would become vulnerable to competitors and customers. This, in turn, would increase the uncertainty with respect to production schedules, orders to suppliers, and the likelihood of meeting demand. Finally, Prater et al (2001) propose that when faced with the situation, the firm has three choices: (1) the firm can choose to deal with the resulting uncertainty; (2) the firm can choose to implement costly coordination mechanisms; or (3) the firm can limit complexity by restructuring the supply chain.

From the literature reviewed above, the following conclusions can be drawn. First of all, contrary to conventional practice, the understanding of flexibility should not be placed merely on the obvious aspects like machines or technology. Instead, in order to enhance competeveness and effectiveness, a more thorough approach is advised and flexibility should be carried out in a more coherent fashion. Second, it is suggested that flexibility should not be confined into something that happens within a firm dynamics. Instead, it should be something that extends beyond the firm and immerse in other domains of the supply chain, affecting the design of effective supply chain strategies. Third, the definition of SCF is board which includes multiple components, conceptual levels and theoretical details. In this case, it is not recommended viewing SCF simply as a reactive means to cope with diversity and uncertainly, but a salient aspect of supply chain management. Last but not least, a firm's capability on SCF is likely to have a positive correlation towards the firm's performance; SCF should be incorporated when designing strategies for enhancing performance.

Based on the conclusions above, a list of potential research questions with respect to the concept of supply chain flexibility and firm performance are suggested below:

1. Does increasing environmental uncertainty result in a greater emphasis on a particular component of supply chain flexibilities? If it does, how to we decide the priority of such emphasis and how do we measure the subsequent performance?
2. Does greater strategic emphasis or performance on one dimension of supply chain flexibility naturally result in greater emphasis or performance on other dimensions? What would be the cost of such strategic emphasis and how do we measure it?
3. Does greater strategic emphasis on one particular supply chain flexibilities promotes a radiating effect where higher performance on other dimensions is obtained?
4. Does better performance on supply chain flexibility dimensions bring forth better overall firm performance? How do we measure and substantiate such better performance?
5. Do high performers on the various dimensions of supply chain flexibility depend on different organizational configurations? Are there prominent variables that go across the board for

better   control   of   the   firm's   performance?

One interesting aspect of the study of SFC is linked to the measurement of supply chain performance.   Nearly all the questions depicted above require a certain degree of measurement in order to evaluate either the effectiveness of supply chain strategies or the performance of a firm's supply chain management. The process of choosing appropriate supply chain performance measures is by all means difficult if not controversial due to the complexity of these systems. A future direction towards evaluating and measuring supply chain performance in relation with SCF would be looking at the selection of performance measurement components.   These components should constitute measurement systems for supply chains of different sectors. The process should than involve a process of differentiating which factors of performance measures are identified as necessary components in any supply chain. In the long run, research can be done to build up performance measurement systems for any given supply chain serving as criteria reference.

References

Beamon, B. M. (1999). Measuring supply chain performance. *International Journal of Operations & Production Management*, 19(3), 275-292.

Calantone, R., & Dröge, C. (2006). Supply chain flexibility: an empirical study. *Journal of Supply Chain Management*, 35(3), 16-24.

Duclos, L. K., Vokurka, R. J., & Lummus, R. R. (2003). A conceptual model of supply chain flexibility. *Industrial Management & Data Systems*, 103(6), 446-456.

Grigore, S. D. (2007). Supply chain flexibility. *Romanian Economic Business Review*, 2(1), 66-70.

Prater, E., Biehl, M., & Smith, M. A. (2001). International supply chain agility-Tradeoffs between flexibility and uncertainty. *International Journal of Operations & Production Management*, 21(5/6), 823-839.

Sánchez, A. M., & Pérez, M. P. (2005). Supply chain flexibility and firm performance: a conceptual model and empirical study in the automotive industry. *International Journal of Operations & Production Management*, 25(7), 681-700.

Simchi-Levi, D., Kaminsky, P., & Simchi-Levi, E.(2008). *Designing and Managing the Supply Chain: Concepts, Strategies and Case Studies*, 3rd edition, McGraw-Hill,

Stevenson, M., & Spring, M. (2007). Flexibility from a supply chain perspective: definition and review. *International Journal of Operations & Production Management*, 27(7), 685-713.

Vickery, S., Calantone, R., & C. Droge, 1999: Supply Chain Flexibility: An Empirical Study, *Journal of Supply Chain Management*; 35:3, ABI/INFORM Global, 25.

Corporate Decision: the Case of Disney's Eisner and Ovitz

The truth is the only way that we can get anywhere. Because any decision-making that is based upon lies or ignorance can't lead to a good conclusion.

-Julian Assange

While it is not without despondence that heroes may not appear in every story; there would certainly be victims when there is no hero but villain, exacerbated when there is not just one, but a double-team of villains. The case of Eisner-Ovitz shows that when people (Disney's board members) are bestowed with the power to make crucial decisions which could affect the welfare of innocent people (shareholders), there is little reason, not even legal one, which could prevent these decision makings to run amuck resulting in people eventually being victimized. The present paper thus aims to analyze the decision making process involved in the case of Eisner-Ovitz with an attempt to propose preventive measures as to how shareholders may be better protected in future. The present paper first provides a summary of the case with an emphasis on the key issues identified, the underlying problem and the subsequent impacts. Next, social identity theory and social categorization theory will be adopted to analyze the decision making processes involved in the case. The writer will proceed to propose preventive solutions to the problems and a conclusion will then be followed.

In 1995, Disney's board members allowed Chairman Michael Eisner to hire his former pal Michael Ovitz as president. After a tumultuous 14 months as Eisner's second in command, Ovitz was forced out by Eisner in January 1997 and left Disney with a $140 million severance package. While Eisner assumed the role of being disinterested as chairman, the majority of Disney's directors who were independent in principle had some sort of personal connections with Eisner. Shareholders were furious and sued Eisner and Disney's directors for untenably awarding Ovitz with such unreasonable severance package. After months of legal wrangling and millions spent in legal processing, one after another stand-off dramas between one rich, powerful guy to another rich, powerful guy, in 2005, the Delaware courts upheld Disney's payment and ruled that the directors did not breach duties of due care and good faith. The fundamental implication of the case lies with the differentiation between what constitutes principles of corporate law and what is considered to be desirable or aspirational practices in the corporate world (Lederman, 2007). In spite of the fact that Delaware courts let down the plaintiffs, the courts had been describing the duties of due care, loyalty, and good faith in terms of the Business Judgment Rules, with the jurisprudence of good faith being the less established one (Gold, 2012).

The key issues involved in the case of Eisner-Ovitz were whether the practices of Disney's directors had breached the duties of due care and good faith (Gold, 2012; Powell, 2007). To establish a breach of the duties of due care the plaintiffs must establish gross negligence of the director's actions that they had fallen outside the bounds of reasons. But in order to establish that, the courts would need to second-guess the judgments of the directors which they were reluctant to engage (Powell, 2007). At the same time, to establish a breach of the duties of good faith, the courts would need an explicit definition on hand in order to prove otherwise that the directors' decisions were not made in good faith (Powell,

2007). While the paper does not seek to argue against the legal viewpoints of the Delaware courts, the paper is inclined to believe that the case of Eisner-Ovitz was a clear example of corporate malpractice which resulted in a loss of valuable resources and welfare of shareholders and relevant stakeholders. What is ironic is that while factual consequence of loss is observable in this case, it is not that obvious to point out that the actions of Disney's directors were against popular corporate social responsibly (CSR) guidelines. Referring to Carroll (1983)'s definition, for example, being the most widely accepted and cited definition of CSR (Crane & Matten, 2004), it is noted that:

> The conduct of a business so that it is economically profitable, law abiding, ethical and socially supportive. To be socially responsible then means that profitability and obedience to the law are foremost conditions when discussing the firm's ethics and the extent to which it supports the society in which it exists with contributions of money, time and talent (p. 608)

According to such definition, not only legally Disney's directors had no qualms in their decision making, such acts were not even a violation of CSR guidelines, at least of the one as defined by Carroll (1983), inasmuch the antecedent premises were that Disney had indeed been making profits and had indeed not been violating any legal regulations. Hence, we could only argue ethically with rational of Jeremy Bentham[2] which human activity was driven by only two motivating forces—the avoidance of pain and the pursuit of pleasure, and all social and political decisions should be made with the aim of achieving the greatest happiness for the greatest number of people. In this light, hence, considering that there will still likely be comparable environmental constraints as discussed, with respect to Herbert Simon's (1972) theory of bounded rationality, the approaches for generating "acceptable solutions" (instead of optimized solutions) to the problem would

[2] Jeremy Bentham (1748-1832), British philosopher, jurist, and social reformer, regarded as the founder of modern utilitarianism.

be: first, understanding why directors would make or support decisions which could go against shareholders' will if theoretically the directors were accountable and liable to shareholders' welfare. Second, how this could be prevented so that shareholders would better be protected in future. For the first question, the paper will proceed to analyze the decision making processes of the directors from the perspective of social identity theory.

British social psychologist Henri Tajfel (1919-1982) in collaboration with his graduate student John Turner (1947-2011) pioneered the social identity approach which comprises social identity theory (Tajfel & Turner, 1979) and self-categorisation theory (Tajfel, Billig, Bundy & Flament, 1971; Turner 1985; Turner et al, 1987). In the scope of the present case study, it helps explain how Disney directors see and define themselves as being a social member of the Disney Board. According the theory, social identity is a person's perception of oneself in relationship with the social aggregations which the person participates in and belongs to. While social identity helps define the identity of oneself, it also has the adaptive function of fabricating social behaviour (Turner, 1984). The social identity approach suggests that human interaction ranges on a broad spectrum where it is 'interpersonal' on the one hand and 'intergroup' on the other. A purely interpersonal interaction, considered rare by Tajfel and Turner, involves people relating entirely on an individual basis. In contrast, when a person's idiosyncratic qualities are overwhelmed by the salience of the person's group memberships, a purely intergroup interaction is to take place where the person relate entirely as a member of his or her groups. Therefore, Disney directors were likely to consider themselves as one intergroup which shared the same social identity.

A more in-depth observation of group membership and the way

individuals perceive such classification of groups leads to the discourse of social categorization theory. According to social categorization theory, individuals have the tendency to classify people including themselves into various social categories (Tajfel & Turner, 1985). Social categorization is the grouping of diverse social circles based on the members' stereotypical attributes, culture, background and behaviour. People may choose to adopt different categorization schemas while they are being classified in a wide range of social categories. People are therefore being assigned with the prototypical characteristics of the category to which they have been segmented and classified. Therefore, Disney's directors may consider themselves and other directors to be classified as one in intergroup of the 'board of Disney'; each director within the board shared mutual qualities which could reinforce the entire group identity.

The interplay of social identity along with social categories naturally leads to the dynamics of 'in-groups' and 'out-groups'. An in-group is a term which refers to a social group to which a person conceptually identifies as being a member. By contrast, an out-group is a social group with which an individual does not identify. In-groups and out-groups bring about the mechanism of social comparison where people compare in-group members with out-group members and look for motivators and benefits to be incorporated within the in-group which enhances self-esteem. Positive distinctiveness, therefore, is generated in situations where individuals use verbal or non-verbal cues to make the group they belong to more socially valued, creating an increasingly positive meaning and favouritism for the identity of the group. Therefore, Disney board of directors and Eisner were likely to have displayed a collective favouritism during the hiring of Ovitz when the in-group is more approximate to their self-definition and the process of social comparison is reinforced. Nonetheless, when Ovitz was fired by Eisner, he was likely to have been 'cast out' and considered as an out-group by the whole board regardless of whatever personal issues Eisner had with him. In other words, Eisner somehow encouraged his in-group to come together in a collective decision making mode, during the hiring and firing of Ovitz, which rationality was bounded by the cognitive biases of group identity, category and dynamics. It goes without saying because shareholders were definitely an out-group to Eisner and the board of directors, their benefits and welfare would be least concerned. Assuming the case to be grimmer, should the out-group be considered as low-status group (shareholders), the high-status comparison group (board of directors) may be relatively unconcerned about such comparisons and form no strong impression about the low-status group. As observed by Ashforth & Mael (1989), such indifference of the high-status group is the greatest threat to the identity of the low-status group because their identity and welfare remain socially invalidated which, therefore, explains why the impact of such decisions toward shareholders being unconcerned by the decision makers.

The analysis above suggests the followings: first, social identity of the board of directors intervened with the decision making they had on the hiring and firing of Ovitz. Second, the interference of decision making was likely to be an example of bounded rationality with respect to cognitive biases caused by group identity and dynamics. Third, the interplay of in-group and out-group which results in group favoritism played a main factor in the case of Eisner and Ovitz. In this connection, the writer recommends a more vigilant corporate monitoring by establishing an appropriate supervisory and compliance structure which aims to: first, create a sophisticated inventory of regulatory focus which faced by the firm's independence, transparency and fairness of decision making. Second, implement an "early warning" system to track and identify emerging areas of regulatory deviation and defectiveness. Third, maintain constant communication between the board and senior management; divulge compliance messages throughout the organization and form it as a salient aspect of corporate culture. Fourth, conduct specialized training for supervisors for their awareness of bounded rationality with respect to group identity, decision making processes and impacts. Finally, ensure that information concerning regulatory and reputational risks and issues is promptly surfaced to CSR compliance by senior management and compliance personnel, putting shareholder and stakeholder needs and welfare as priority.

In conclusion, the present paper attempted to analyze the case of Eisner-Ovitz by adopting social identity and social categorization theory. The present paper argued that the decision making process of the Disney's board of directors experienced bounded rationality with cognitive biases derived by group identity, categorization and dynamics. The writer of the paper proposed that in order to rectify the problem and help shareholders be better protected in future, a vigilant regulatory system should be implanted, so that the decision making process should be one that is as transparent and independent as possible.

Reference

Ashforth, B. E., & Mael, F. (1989). Social identity theory and the organization. *Academy of management review,* 14(1), 20-39.

Carroll, A. B. (1983). Corporate social responsibility: Will industry respond to cut-backs in social program funding? *Vital Speeches of the Day,* 49, p. 604-608.

Crane, A. & Matten, D. (2004). *Business Ethics.* Oxford: Oxford University Press.

Gold, A. S. (2007). A Decision Theory Approach to the Business Judgment Rule: Reflections on Disney, Good Faith, and Judicial Uncertainty, 66 *Md. L. Rev.*

398.

Lederman, L. (2007). Disney Examined; A Case Study in Corporate Governance and CEO Succession. *NYL Sch. L. Rev., 52,* 557.

Powell, W. J. (2006). Corporate Governance and Fiduciary Duty: The Mickey Mouse Rule or Legal Consistency, Protection of Shareholder Expectations, and Balanced Director Autonomy. *Geo. Mason L. Rev., 14,* 799.

Simon, H. A. (1972). Theories of bounded rationality. Decision and organization, 1, 161-176.

Tajfel, H., Billig, M. G., Bundy, R. P., & Flament, C. (1971). Social categorization and intergroup behaviour. *European Journal of Social Psychology,* 1(2), 149-178.

Tajfel, H., & Turner, J.C. (1979). An integrative theory of inter-group conflict. In W.G. Austin & S. Worchel (Eds.), *The Social Psychology of Intergroup Relations* (pp. 33–47). Monterey, CA: Brooks/Cole.   (used again in uncertainty)

Tajfel, H., & Turner, J. C. (1985). The social identity theory of intergroup behavior. In S. Worchel & W. G. Austin (Eds.), *Psychology of intergroup relations* (2nd ed., pp. 7-24). Chicago: Nelson-Hall.

Turner, J.C. (1984). Social identification and psychological group formation In H. Tajfel (Ed.), *The Social Dimension* (Vol. 2, pp. 518–538). Cambridge: Cambridge University Press.

Turner, J. C. (1985) Social categorization and the selfconcept: A social cognitive theory of group behavior. In E. J. Lawler (Ed.), *Advances in group processes* (Vol. 2, pp. 77-122). Greenwich, CT: JAI Press.

Ethical Human Resource Practice: the Case of Nike

Great vision without great people is irrelevant.
- Jim Collins

The very term "Corporate Social Responsibility" (CSR) advocates an organizational shift of focus which orientates business organizations to go beyond being profitable and obeying all laws, and be committed in avoiding questionable practices and striving for being a "good corporate citizen" (Roberts, Keeble & Brown, 2002; Nelson, 2005; Matten & Crane, 2005). With regard to the importance of protecting the welfare of employees at work, nonetheless, there is a divergence of opinion among commentators: some argue that with respect to CSR, organisations catering to the needs of employees being the key stakeholders not only is moral but promotes sustainability. Conservatively, others argue that catering to the needs of employees is simply a means to achieve the best consequence of being profitable.

Regardless of which of these claims is more relevant to today's business environment, a central conviction points to the ground that the drive to maximize long-term profits naturally overlaps with the imperative to treat employees justly. The present paper however sees that such shared conviction is palpably at odds as suggested from the evidence from the real business world. The present paper therefore attempts to use the case of Nike to examine the following three questions: Can the interest of employees and the interests of business really coincide? What happens when they are in conflict? And what role should HR managers take when they do? In the following sections, the

73

paper will discuss facts discovered, ideas generated, and advice made based on these core issues.

Nike, being one of the world's top sports clothing brand, has been alleged of sweatshops and child labour. In the process of outsourcing manufacturing, Indonesian workers of Nike's contractors have been physically and mentally abused. While working conditions are seriously pitiable, money made by these workers are at the bare minimal (Appendix II). Despite Nike being willing to disclose names and locations of its 'problematic' production plants after years of criticism, no imminent solutions have been implemented.

Regarding the definition of ethics, Stone(2014) describes ethics to be associated with morality and standards of behaviour and may require higher standards than that established by laws. Carroll, & Buchholtz(2012) argue that ethics refers to issues of right, wrong, fairness, and justice; business ethics has to do with ethical issues that arise in the commercial realm.

Looking at the relationship between HRM practices and ethics, Winstanley and Woodall (2000) describe HRM practices to be a trend increasingly challenged by researchers from a more critical and ethical perspective; HRM practices and policies affect employee's experiences of work and the employment relationship. Looking at the definition of CSR, Carroll (1983) offers the classic definition of CSR as:

> The conduct of a business so that it is economically profitable, law abiding, ethical and socially supportive. To be socially responsible then means that profitability and obedience to the law are foremost conditions when discussing the firm's ethics and the extent to which it supports the society in which it exists with contributions of money, time and talent (p. 608)

Finally, the three approaches to industrial relationships are: a. The unitarist approach, b. The pluralist approach, and c. The radical/Marxist approach. The unitarist approach assumes that industrial relationship is grounded in mutual cooperation and the sharing common objectives. In contrast, the pluralist approach regards employers and employees to be individuals and conflict is inevitably due to conflicting interests. Similarly, the radical or Marxist approach also assumes that conflict is inevitable, yet, the root of conflict has more to do with class conflict between the powered and the inferior.

The case of Nike echoes many similar cases where neither the traditional CSR assumption nor the conservative utilitarian assumption of protecting the welfare of employees is sustained. For obvious reasons, the company is making good profit, particularly with lower cost labour, and on the other side of the supply chain, customers could not care less whether they company is 'moral'. As mentioned, no imminent solutions are available, because in terms of the unitarist approach, no reconciliation is feasible to occur; setting up employee's union and treat industrial relationship is impossible as advocated by the pluralist approach, inasmuch the industrial relationships underlying the case of Nike, as Provis (1996) noted, are not simply bounded by 'interest'---of the conflict of it, but also fabricated by values and cultural notions. The only remaining option is likely to be social and political revolutions but this is beyond the scope of the present paper.

Nevertheless, the writer believes in a moral way of doing business and therefore offers a proposal acceptable for big companies like Nike to consider. The aim of the proposal is not to rectify the problem instantly, yet, a reduction of exploitation is expected. When it comes to implementing the proposal with a mission, Nankervis, Compton, Baird, and Coffey (2011) suggest that integrity, legality, proficiency, professional loyalty, and confidentiality are the five ethical dimensions in human resources management. "Integrity", for example, requires the mangers to practice the profession in human resources management with high levels of fairness and honesty. When it comes to carrying out the mission, the company may establish a position of Ethics Officer whose role is to oversee investigations of wrongdoing and coping with ethical issues with senior management (Adobor, 2006).

The writer advises the Ethics Officer to consider the resistance and challenge of carrying out Ethics Policies in the TRIPOD analysis, i.e., industrial, resources and institution analyses as depicted by Peng (2009). For instance, in terms of industry analysis, what can the company do to tackle with the very high bargaining power of outsourcing manufacturers? Can the outsourcing manufacturers be 'penalized' in case unjust treatment of the employees is observed? At the resource level, will the company be able to expand its capabilities in achieving above average return not solely relying on factors like reducing production cost? Is it possible for the company to better prioritize and develop tactics where HR resources are better managed and protected in a given period of time? Finally, in the institutional level, will the company be able to legally infiltrate representatives directly supervised under the Ethics Officers in overseeing the outsourcing production processes? These are questions all worth to be considered and explored in future studies.

References

Adobor, H. (2006). Exploring the role performance of corporate ethics officers. *Journal of Business Ethics, 69*(1), 57-75.

Carroll, A. B. (1983). Corporate social responsibility: Will industry respond to cut-backs in social program funding? *Vital Speeches of the Day,* 49, p. 604-608.

Carroll, A., & Buchholtz, A. (2012).*Business and Society - Ethics and Stakeholder Management*, 7ᵗʰEdition, South-Western Cengage

Nankervis, A. R., Compton, R. L., Baird, M., and Coffey, J. (2011). *Human Resource Management: Strategies & Practice (7ᵗʰed.)*. Victoria: Cengage Learning Australia.

Nelson, J. (2005). Corporate citizenship in a global context. CSRI Working Paper, 13, Harvard University.

Peng, Mike W. (2009) *Global Strategy*, 2nd Edition South-Western – CENGAGE Learning

Roberts, S., Keeble, J., & Brown, D. (2002).*The business case for corporate citizenship*. Arthur D. Little, Ltd., Cambridge, UK, 8.

Provis, C. (1996). Unitarism, pluralism, interests and values. *British Journal of Industrial Relations*, *34*(4), 473-495.

Stone, R. J. (2014).*Human Resource Management* 8ᵗʰEdition, Wiley, 9781742166841 Matten, D., & Crane, A. (2005). Corporate citizenship: toward an extended theoretical conceptualization. *Academy of Management review*, 30(1), 166-179.

Winstanley, D., and Woodall, J. (2000).The ethical dimension of human resource management, *Human Resource Management Journal* 10(2), 5-20.

www.ingramcontent.com/pod-product-compliance
Lightning Source LLC
Chambersburg PA
CBHW070916180526
45168CB00005B/2030